Asperger Syndrome Employment Workbook

of related interest

Asperger's Syndrome
A Guide for Parents and Professionals
Tony Attwood
Foreword by Lorna Wing
ISBN 1 85302 577 1 pb

Pretending to be Normal
Living with Asperger's Syndrome
Liane Holliday Willey
Foreword by Tony Attwood
ISBN 1 85302 749 9 pb

Asperger Syndrome in the Family
Redefining Normal
Liane Holliday Willey
ISBN 1 85302 873 8 pb

Asperger Syndrome Employment Workbook

An employment workbook for adults
with Asperger Syndrome

Roger N. Meyer

Foreword by Tony Attwood

Jessica Kingsley Publishers
London and Philadelphia

First published in the United Kingdom and United States of America in 2001 by
Jessica Kingsley Publishers Ltd,
116 Pentonville Road, London
N1 9JB, England
and
325 Chestnut Street,
Philadelphia, PA 19106, USA.

www.jkp.com

© Copyright 2001 Roger N. Meyer
Foreword © Copyright 2001 Tony Attwood

Library of Congress Cataloging in Publication Data

Meyer, Roger N., 1942–
Asperger employment guide : a workbook for individuals on the autistic spectrum, their families, and helping professionals / Roger N. Meyer.
      p.   cm.
Includes bibliographical references and index.
ISBN 1-85302-796-0 (alk. paper)
1. Vocational guidance for the handicapped problems, exercises, etc. 2. Asperger syndrome--Patients--Vocational guidance.
3. Autism--Patients--Vocational guidance. I. Title.
HV1568.5.M48   1999   99-41650
650.14'087--dc21   CIP

British Library Cataloguing in Publication Data

Meyer, Roger N.
Asperger employment guide : a workbook for individuals on the autistic spectrum, their families, and helping professionals
1. Asperger syndrome - Patients - Employment 2. Asperger syndrome - Popular works 3. Vocational guidance for the handicapped
I. Title
331.5'94
ISBN 1853027960

ISBN 1 85302 796 0

Printed and Bound in Great Britain by
Athenaeum Press, Gateshead, Tyne and Wear

This book is dedicated to the memory of Melvin B. Goldberg, my closest friend from high school and college. A giant of a man in every way, Mel's love of the law, his passion for teaching and unrequited search for truth, justice, and human dignity enriched the lives of all he touched.

Contents

PART 3: The Workbook

Foreword

Roger Meyer is someone who understands the unusual profile of abilities of adults with Asperger Syndrome from personal experience and meticulous study. He was diagnosed relatively late in life and his employment workbook is based on his own work history and the observations and detailed analysis of over 200 adults who have written their employment biographies. The workbook was designed to be read by an adult with Asperger Syndrome and is written in the style of a conversation between author and reader. Roger states 'My interest lies in helping you understand how you arrive at your own decisions'. Completing the workbook is a private journey of discovery that will enable the reader to identify and understand their strengths and weaknesses, resolve issues in their work history and outline a plan for a more successful future.

We have several publications on strategies to help children with Asperger Syndrome at school but Roger's workbook is the seminal publication for adults in the workplace. The challenges faced by such individuals do not end when they leave school, and the development of employment skills and vocational guidance should commence in early adolescence and continue throughout the person's working life. Their profile of abilities can include attributes such as an extensive knowledge base, reliability and attention to detail but a difficulty coping with change, the interpersonal aspects of the position and an unusual learning style. New research is suggesting that adults with Asperger Syndrome can achieve, maintain and succeed in a wide range of occupations but the first step on the journey is to identify their qualities and areas that need to be addressed. This workbook provides that first step.

We recognize the value of work not simply as a source of income for financial independence, but also as a means of improving our self-image, contributing to our community and providing opportunities for social experiences. People with Asperger Syndrome often define themselves primarily by their occupation and interests, i.e. what they do in a practical sense rather than their social network. Unemployment or misery in their job has a devastating effect on their quality of life, self-image and mood. Work circumstances can be a cause of depression, anxiety and anger that require psychological intervention and medication. Improving the person's work circumstances can have a beneficial effect for the individual, their family, colleagues and employer as well as contributing to an improvement in their productivity.

The first part of the workbook provides a review of our knowledge of Asperger Syndrome and aspects relevant to employment. The description of the learning and social profile is particularly illuminating. The reader identifies the characteristics that are applicable to their own profile of abilities as part of the process of self-discovery to make better decisions. However, once the person recognizes their differences, they are faced with the dilemma of disclosure. Who do you inform? How much do you reveal? And what are the likely consequences? Roger outlines the diagnostic process, issues related to disclosure and the importance of self-advocacy. His role is that of a mentor, providing information on employment law, social skills, learning and work styles, conditions associated with Asperger Syndrome as well as special skills and interests.

Roger is a cabinetmaker and his skills are apparent in the meticulous detail and quality of workmanship he provides in the instructions for the employment biography provided in Part 2 of the workbook. He carefully guides the reader through the various stages in completing their employment biography, anticipating their questions and providing answers and examples. Gradually the reader discovers their pattern of abilities, appropriate strategies and accommodations they have used in the past and is helped to develop a comprehensive plan to improve their current and future work.

Although the book is written as a personal self-help manual, it is also designed as a resource for conventional training and employment services. The workbook can also be used by high school teachers preparing the adolescent for the transition between school and work and employment and vocational counselors who are assisting the person to determine an appropriate career and employer. Management and personnel staff will benefit from the information when reviewing deployment and promotion with the person with Asperger Syndrome. It is also a valuable resource for a parent or partner to facilitate wise decisions that will affect the family, and for clinicians who recognize the importance of the person's employment circumstances as a significant factor contributing to their quality of life and mood. Completing Roger Meyer's *Asperger Syndrome Employment Workbook* starts a journey of self-discovery that will have a beneficial effect for all of us.

Tony Attwood
November 2000

Introduction

This is a book for adults with Asperger Syndrome (AS). It addresses one of the most important activities of adulthood: work. Part 1 of this book contains text information about Asperger Syndrome and what is known of its connection to work. Part 2 contains instructions on how to compose an employment biography using the third part of this book. Part 3 is a workbook. The workbook consists of questions that will enable the reader to write an abbreviated or a longer employment biography.

If you are a person with AS, the workbook parts can act as a personal evaluation and planning tool to help you review your past work, a current job, and/or future employment. Once you complete the workbook – even an abbreviated version of it – you may understand the intimate connection between your unique 'flavor' of AS and your work life.

This is a book about change. Although its prime purpose is to be a workbook intended for use by AS adults, special education transition team members can also use it as a reference and guide for adolescents and young adults. Students considering the world of work, whether immediately out of secondary school or beyond, may find it to be of value in reviewing how they learn and how they might respond to employment-related learning situations.

Employment and career counseling professionals, vocational rehabilitation counselors and other professionals may find portions of this book useful when working with clients diagnosed with Asperger Syndrome.

Clinicians consulted by clients diagnosed with AS experiencing specific employment challenges may also find portions of this book of use in helping their clients become more aware of job stressors, possible adaptations, accommodations and alternative solutions. Employee Assistance Program (EAP) and employer human resource personnel may find sections useful in understanding employees who have disclosed their disability and seek reasonable accommodations under provisions of national or local disability discrimination laws. Family members and relations will also find valuable information that will extend their knowledge and understanding.

Many adults with mild forms of AS do succeed at work. Many more do not. AS remains a 'hidden disability' to others, but not to us. It is also a pervasive condition. This means we can't compartmentalize our lives with the hope that AS will be kept at bay. We may try to forget that 'it' is there, but under certain conditions our AS keeps popping up. Sometimes we can anticipate those conditions and avoid them. Other times our characteristics show up as unanticipated and uninvited guests. Keeping our most challenging behaviors hidden or under control exacts an enormous toll on our life outside of work. Many of us are workaholics. Many working AS adults report that we 'have no life' outside of work. When we say this to others, our statements appear to be exaggerations. That is the way others see it. We know differently.

Like other non-AS working adults, we accept the fact that work is often unpleasant. We bitch and moan about it just like NT (neurotypical) folks. There's one important difference: NTs aren't totally consumed by these concerns. Somehow, they manage to break free of their ruminations and get on with their lives.

Many of us don't, and it shows. We are told not to take the things that concern us so seriously. We are told that our negativism can do us in at work. Sometimes it does.

Many NTs work so that they can afford to play. They work hard in order to play hard. Some of them don't work very hard, but they still play hard anyway. Many of us work very hard just to stay afloat, just to survive. If we manage to make time to play we consider ourselves lucky. As young persons, many of us didn't learn that play has an intrinsic value in our lives. While playtime is 'down time' it is also time for recharging our batteries to meet the stresses of life.

Work can be one of the stresses of life.

Stress at work: Some examples

The examples below aren't set out to make you feel bad or hopeless about yourself. They are featured here to illustrate real life situations reported in private correspondence and subscription listservs on the Internet by AS workers. They are here to show you that you have company – you are not the only one. The outcomes? They are real as well. The purpose of this book is to help you avoid those outcomes. Learning what *not* to do may be the first lesson in learning what to do to survive and flourish in the workforce.

You don't understand the social rules of the work environment. You don't understand personal space, what is private and what isn't. You don't know what topics are appropriate or even realize 'who you are talking to'.

Result: Complaints of harassment by you against others, or others against you; complaints that you aren't a team player, and that you'd better straighten up and fly right. *Further results:* demotion, suspension, or termination.

You lose your temper – or hold it in – and are angry much of the time.

Result: Warnings about your anger and your outbursts or sullenness. Supervisors and fellow workers say you are creating a hostile work environment.

You feel so exhausted daily just from 'hanging on' or controlling yourself that you arrive home drained, virtually unable to function. You need a full recharge of your batteries just to face the next day.

Result: You don't have time for family, intimate relationships, friendship and other diverse interests to balance your life outside of work. You realize you are working just to work.

People at work consider you arrogant and a know-it-all. You are proud of your knowledge, and you don't know how to 'hold back'. You go on and on, and people have to cut you off or tell you to stop.

Result: Repeated warnings that you interfere with other's work by taking too much of their time. *Further results:* In response to such criticism, you find yourself 'doing it again'. On the other hand, you might withdraw and become 'distant' from your work colleagues. *Possible final results:* Others avoid you, or you are moved to an assignment way from the others, end up at a job nobody wants with the anticipation of all that you will quit. If you don't 'take the hint' you may be fired.

You have difficulty asking for help with a problem or a work issue, or by the time you do ask, things have 'gone too far'.

Result: Others are increasingly concerned about your performance. *Another result:* Your co-workers become uncomfortable about helping you because you appear so globally needy once you finally ask for help. *Ultimate result:* The boss tells you that you don't appear to be learning fast enough or are repeating the same requests for help too often – warning, layoff, or firing.

You know you can learn the job or the task. However, you are not provided with information that fits your learning style, and so you bumble along, always stressed. You also fear being given new tasks you aren't ready to handle. You avoid promotions because you fear having to supervise others. You think that if you can't learn something yourself, you can't teach others.

Results: Your supervisor calls you a slow learner. He thought you had promise. Your supervisor or others monitor your performance frequently. You feel rushed much of the time. You feel that everyone else is aware of your problem. You mistake unsolicited help offered by others for criticism. You don't handle criticism well. You withdraw or your fellow workers withdraw from you. You know it's just a matter of time before you are asked to leave. You quit or are fired.

You have difficulty being assertive. You feel your assertiveness will be mistaken for aggressiveness. Therefore, you remain passive, but not all the time.

Result: You feel misunderstood. You don't feel comfortable following others' advice about your being a self-advocate. You let things 'slip by' or you feel walked all over or ignored. You become vigilant and silently resentful. *Another result:* Your irritation 'spills out' when you can't stand being ignored or abused any longer. After these outbursts, you feel better. You even apologize. You know this will happen again, and so do your fellow workers. *Ultimate result:* Your passiveness or assertiveness becomes a discipline issue. You are warned to get yourself under control. You promise to do so, but you 'can't'. Further discipline follows, with demotion, reassignment, or termination.

You know that some work challenges are directly related to your Asperger Syndrome. Should you disclose your diagnosis, and to whom? How much do you say, when do you do it, and what do you think your disclosure will accomplish?

Result: You remain in a quandary. Maybe you don't say anything and you commit yourself to that stance. Maybe you tell someone, and that person turns out to be the wrong person. Maybe you wait too long. When you explain yourself in a disciplinary or supervisory session, what you say and how you say it sounds like an excuse and not an explanation. The supervisor has a bad reaction to what you say. After the event, you 'know' your days are numbered. Maybe you quit. Maybe you are fired.

To avoid all of the above, you seek jobs or are placed in jobs where you are underemployed. You take a job that is 'any job' just to keep working. You have a work history of many jobs, and you can't seem to hold onto a job even though you have a good interview technique.

Result: You feel lousy about your work and your work history. You might be a steady worker, but that's all, and for many employers, that isn't enough. You don't know how call attention to yourself without seeming to brag. You are sometimes abused because of your 'lowly' position. Sometimes you want to tell people you are more capable, but you don't. *Ultimate result:* You feel depressed and unappreciated. As a part of the small talk with people, they ask you what you do. You tell them that you are 'just' a lowly worker. That isn't the answer they expected to hear. Nevertheless, you hear yourself saying it a lot, and then you start to believe it. Then you get more depressed. Maybe you start to drink or abuse drugs to take the edge off the pain. Maybe you get sick a lot and miss work. Now you've got a double problem. And you've got a 'reputation'.

The broader issues

Sometimes, people just have to stop and think about work. Maybe you've concluded that your present work doesn't pay you enough. It may be so personally distasteful that keeping your job isn't an option. Sometimes, events force you to reconsider your line of work, such as when you are injured or when your skills are no longer needed because the work itself has changed. Maybe you need to learn new work skills to get a job or remain employable.

You might have just received your AS diagnosis and have some serious thinking to do. You might be considering an entitlement program as the best alternative to a presently impossible employment situation. On the other hand, if you are in an entitlement program such as Social Security you know that there is work for you beyond a part-time, limited-income job and a government check. You are tired of other people making decisions for you.

Problems such as those outlined in the examples above may be no strangers to you. Perhaps you have major performance or efficiency concerns. Perhaps you've 'burned through' every employer in your line of work. Perhaps you've exhausted every rehabilitation or training program that others have set out for you. Your spouse, partner or friends may have told you to either face your work problems or face separation, divorce, or loss of their friendship. Or, you may simply feel like a square peg in a round hole and nothing you've tried so far seems to fit. You may not have encountered any large problems, but the small problems are killing you. You feel you aren't making use of your strengths.

Maybe you have existed from crisis to crisis in your work life for so long that you've finally got tired of your own crisis mentality 'running your life.' Now, you want to take charge.

Is it time for you to get off the merry-go-round and recover your balance? Another question: How much more time do you need?

To use a term of the 1960s, you can 'find your own center' by systematically going through the steps of writing your own employment biography using this workbook as a guide. Understanding the connection between your AS and your work life may buy you a ticket to a different ride.

The second part of this book contains instructions and examples of how to answer questions in the third part, the workbook. You, the reader, will provide the answers. Many of the questions appear simple and concrete. That makes sense. We are known as concrete thinkers. As you review your answers, you may begin to reflect thoroughly on your past and present work. By taking the time to think carefully about your answers and by making your own connections between them, you can begin to 'get a handle' on aspects of your work life that have been of concern to you. By completing your employment biography using the workbook as a guide, you can systematically identify and address those issues.

Structure of the book

This book is divided into three parts. Before you start reading the text information found in the first part, I ask you to go through an exercise of listing every job you have ever held, thinking of them in a particular way, and choosing three jobs that represent the 'hooks' on which an employment biography can be written. Even if you intend only to read this book without using it as an employment biographical guide, the reason for going through this exercise will become apparent as you read through the rest of Part 1.

Following the exercise, Part 1 chapters discuss aspects of Asperger Syndrome as they relate to your employment. The first chapter discusses diagnosis, disclosure and self-advocacy. If you are diagnosed with AS you may wish to re-read this chapter before starting to compose your employment history. Part 1 offers information that should provoke self-reflection and your greater awareness of the workplace environment.

Part 2 of the book is the 'How To' part. The introduction to Part 2 explains what tools, supplies and materials you need to write your employment biography. It provides detailed instructions and examples of answers for Part 3 of this book, the workbook.

How this book happened

This book is the direct outgrowth of a failed exploratory research project begun in the fall of 1997, in Portland Oregon. After receiving my diagnosis of AS in July, I set about to discover what research exists on adults with AS. I was especially interested in the world of work, since I knew I was not long to remain a cabinetmaker (a skilled craft I loved in a perverse white knuckled existence for 26 years). I was dismayed to find nothing other than scattered anecdotal journal reports and several personal biographies.

Purblind my entire life to the profound effect AS had upon my work, I sketched out the design of an exploratory research project to study the effect of AS upon the work lives of other mature adults. I was still working as a cabinetmaker, and dreaded the thought of making too many changes at once to my life. Portland Oregon was not known as a center of knowledge in this field, but it seemed as good a place to start as any.

Luckily, I discovered a professional doing serious work as a developmental disabilities family case manager with a local government agency. Her 12-year-old son had Asperger Syndrome, and her concern about the future of her pre-adolescent child appeared to resonate with the broader issues I raised about the future for all adults with AS. She had two professional acquaintances willing to join in discussion.

Academic research by committee has its drawbacks, not the least being the time required for consensus building around the very definition of the project itself. Demonstrating a classic manifestation of my own flavor of AS, I paid little heed to the style and work pace of my colleagues, and soon after launching the project began to leave them behind. They had their own lives and careers beyond this project. Not me. Despite their breathless imprecations to slow down, I allowed my juggernaut to thunder along with a wide-open throttle on its own track.

Within a week of the first meeting of our 'gang of four' in Portland and without advance discussion, I drew together an Internet on-line survey questionnaire work group. With the click of the mouse, the project 'went international'. I had to explain myself to my cautious Portland colleagues conducting exploratory discussions of a research project. Explanations of my many other unilateral excursions became a defining feature of our monthly meetings.

'Why, if we were to do extensive work-history interviews with AS adults in Portland, did I feel impelled to expand the project? Were we not a team, making decisions as a team?'

Explain why a racehorse runs. Fathom the meaning of the personal running of a marathon race. Why climb 'this' mountain? I was driven by an urgent need for answers. From the onset, this was not to be a leisurely ramble. Over the summer of my diagnosis, I had come across others like myself occupying the different space of the Internet. This was a world then unknown to my research colleagues yet one in which I felt at perfect ease. This was a world comprised of mature adults medically or self-diagnosed with AS willing to share our insights with one another without the intervening permission of 'experts'. We shared our work biographies. More than any other factor, I believe this unmoderated intercourse between my diagnosed peers and I threatened my colleagues' sense of control over the project. I was also a loose cannon. There was and still remains something profoundly unsettling in recognizing the impact of being 'differently brained'.[1]

When the on-line group started, I had no idea our discussion would bear fruit so quickly. Animated postings between members of the on-line work group suggested many of the questions in this book. Within two months I completed the outline of a basic instrument for the research project. It was an on-line survey designed to supplement data gathered in the personal interviews of the Portland project. It was impossibly long. As the on-line survey took form I became impatient with the inevitable delays implicit in academic research. At a meeting before summer break, my colleagues allowed me to take my on-line project 'private'. Although this final product bears little resemblance to the version of the survey/questionnaire last shared with my Internet work colleagues, my indebtedness to them is great.

I take full responsibility for the role my impulsiveness played in the ending of one dream and the beginning of another – this book. To those I disappointed by not pursuing the research effort further, I express my apology. To those who encouraged me to complete this book, a project that had taken on a life of its own, I owe a profound debt of gratitude.

For each reader this workbook starts a private journey. Like many other journeys we undertake, this one too is taken alone. As the author, I find it impossible not to want to accompany you, and with your permission, I beg your indulgence in making frequent reference to 'we' or 'us'.

One caveat before we begin. For the purposes of this book, this author joins with an Australian counterpart in considering AS a feature of human neuro-diversity.[2] Viewing ourselves as 'different' is a non-limiting term by which we can consider our capacity to contribute to the richness of our cultural and social fabric. Over the last decade, some persons within the international human rights movement have joined a nascent international disabilities rights movement in a serious effort to dismantle the medical 'disorder' model. Members of the world medical and social services communities recognize the

1   Meyerding, J., (1998) 'Thoughts on finding Myself Differently Brained.' On Independent Living on the Autistic Spectrum, http://www.inlv.demon.nl/subm.brain.jane.eng.html
2   Singer, J. (1998) 'Odd People In.' Unpublished BA Thesis, Faculty of Humanities and Social Science, University of Technology, Sydney, Australia

destructive consequences attendant to retaining the old model, yet appear powerless to shake themselves free of the basic paradigm embracing the terms 'disorder' and 'disability'.[3]

We are neither our disorder nor our disability. Each of us is a whole greater than the sum of any smaller parts experts wish to assign to us.

Thanks

As with any writer's first lengthy publication, this has been a labor of sheer exasperation and love. This work I owe to my parents. As an autodidact, much of what I've learned about Asperger Syndrome has come easily, but not the personal pieces. I was blessed with a mother whose wicked wit and tongue taught me the language I love dearly, and the ways to talk and write myself out of deep trouble and profound, verbally inexpressible pain. My father's AS stoicism and breathless blue temper double scored my wall of defiance and unending rage. This man's troubled protective love for me flickered darkly in his waning years, at last free of his shell of silence and lifelong depression. Only since my diagnosis has understanding allowed me to forge a different memory of him. That memory now rests in a peaceful place in my life, a place he never knew in his.

Thanks to all of my unseen on-line confidants, my colleagues along the way of creating this book. A special thanks to two especially, Patricia Clark and a person whose anonymity still protects her with an on-line pseudonym, the early editors to this venture. Thanks to my former project colleagues in Portland Oregon, whose patience each was thrice that of Job: Phyllis Coyne, M Ed, Ann Fullerton, PhD, and Jane Rake. To my former upstairs neighbors in Portland, Jack Williams and Helen 'Stevie' Chinitz, whose constant encouragement, free dinners, 'test reading indulgences' of snippets here and there, and overall comity have made them my first adult-life friends, my greatest appreciation.

A special thanks goes to Jessica Kingsley, publisher and my editor for making it through the first manuscript, struggling with my disorganized

---

3   See World Health Organization ICIDH-2, (1998) 'International Classification of Impairments, Activities and Participation,' http://www.who.int.msa.mnh.ems.icidh/icidh.htm

'order', and allowing her commissioning editor, Helen Parry, vast amounts of time to put up with my peccadilloes.

Thanks to Doug Prior, illustrator, whose drawings may help writers organize their materials while composing their employment biographies.

Thanks, too, to members of my Portland Asperger Syndrome Support Group, a group I founded and still moderate, whose individual members have been my personal beacons of hope and reminders of the need for dignified adult community self-determination and nurturance.

PART 1

The Issues Involved

CHAPTER I

Three Jobs

This is the only chapter where all readers are asked to do some written work. Even if you go no further than listing all the jobs you have ever held and divide your work life into three periods, you will recognize how rich has been your connection to work.

If you wish to use this book as a personal employment guide and biography, consider your life on a continuum labeled 'work'. As you consider each topic in succeeding chapters to this first part of the book, I ask you to always refer to the three job choices you made as you finished this short chapter. Even if you do not intend to use this book to write your employment history, I request that you consider your life on a work continuum. Doing so will help you follow the author's logic in ordering information found in the succeeding chapters to the first part of this book.

Think of your work life as being divided into three periods. Persons who have worked should have little difficulty identifying three distinct periods of their life as workers. For the purposes of analysis and comparison, I ask you to select one representative job from each of these three periods.

Refer to the first page of Part 3, the workbook. The first section of the workbook is entitled 'Three Jobs'. Note that the first page is blank except for the heading 'All My Jobs'. Starting chronologically from your earliest job, list every job you can recall, ending with your present or last job. List every job regardless of whether you were paid, worked as a volunteer, or were self-employed. In writing this list, do not bother to think whether the job was important. The point is that you held it. Write quickly. Try to finish the list in one sitting. Write job titles using only two or three words at most. Develop your own abbreviated description of the job using words that make sense to you.

After you are done listing all your jobs, use the criteria below in deciding how to divide your work life into three periods.

First period

The first period is a time of your first job or first jobs. It was a time when you learned the value of work by either being paid money or being awarded privileges for accomplishing a job. It was the time when you learned about such things as being on time, following directions and the example of others, and how to relate to fellow workers. It was the time when others knew that what you did was 'work'. This period in your work life could involve just your first job. That would be unusual. Most people are able to identify a few jobs that logically fit into this first period. Some people don't succeed in their first jobs while others do very well. In all cases, these first jobs are an important learning experience.

Middle period

Your next job(s) belong to a 'middle period'. Most likely, this period will match a time of your life just after you finished school. Despite how much work people do before then, many people consider their first job out of high school or college to be very different from jobs they held during their first period. Jobs in the middle period would be paid jobs that supported your independence. Many people identify the start of this period as the time they held their first job away from home, or the first job where the decision to apply for it or accept it was their own and not anyone else's. These are jobs normally associated with the age of young adulthood, from the age of 18 to 25. During this job period, many young adults experiment with their career choice. Middle-period jobs are those you and others regard as 'serious'. The period of experimentation – even with serious jobs – could last well beyond the age of 25.

Late period

If you are a young adult, you may see distinct differences between an early period of young adulthood and a later period of young adulthood. You can identify a job held at the beginning of that period as quite different than a job you hold now, or recently held. Consider that early job a 'middle-period' job, and the last or current job your 'late-period' job.

If you are older than 25, cultural conventions in Western society consider you a mature adult. If you are much older than 25, you could consider jobs held before the age of 30 or 35 as 'middle-period' jobs. As you consider your employment biography, however, you must decide where the dividing line occurred between such a middle-period and the time you consider that of your employment maturity. The jobs between the end of your early-period and the beginning of your time of employment maturity are your middle-period jobs.

If you are near retirement or are retired, your late period of employment could be a period lasting many years. Of the three jobs you choose, this is the only one that you cannot choose from a selection of many in the period. Choose your present job or your most recent as your late-period job.

Now that you understand the difference between each period of work, draw a line on your list separating your first-period and middle-period job(s). Do the same to separate your middle period and your period of employment maturity. In reviewing how you want to break up your periods, you don't have to divide the periods into the same number of years. Also, the periods don't have to agree with any of the other ways you think of your past.

From the complete list, choose one job from each period, and mark it clearly.

As you look in more detail at each of these representative jobs in your life, you will almost certainly be able to construct a complete picture of that job in a way you haven't done in the past. You will be thinking about similarities as well as differences between your job experiences. By distinguishing the differences between your past jobs, you can avoid making overgeneralizations about yourself as a worker. Understanding each of your choices as representative of a certain period of your work history may help you to seek a better fit for yourself in your current and future work. You will know what to look for in a job you are considering and what questions to ask of a new employer. For any job situation, present or future, completing this book will help you identify caution signals as well as green lights. For the moment, choose your three jobs, and then continue reading the first part of this book.

If you choose to complete the workbook, you will have a chance to reconsider your choice of the first two jobs before you begin to answer questions in Part 3.

CHAPTER 2

Diagnosis, Disclosure and Self-advocacy

Bleuler coined the term 'autistic' in 1911 to describe a form of self-absorbed behavior of persons labeled as psychotic. These psychiatric patients lacked some of the severe pathologies associated with morally objectionable adult conduct. In 1943, Leo Kanner, an American child psychiatrist, adopted Bleuler's term in describing behaviors of children we now consider 'low functioning'. A year later, a young psychiatrist in Vienna working at an institute that we would now call a developmental disabilities clinic used Bleuler's term to describe four boys whose behavior was at the opposite end of the functional continuum. Neither man knew the other, but both were on to something. The wartime publication of Kanner's paper remained somewhat of a secret for the next 15 years. Asperger's paper fared even worse. It remained unnoticed for nearly 40 years. Following the publication of his wartime article, Asperger turned his attention to other child development issues.

After the war, psychiatry was in a state of flux. Doctors treating children and adults who had undergone the traumas of wartime experienced inconsistent results in their efforts to treat the victims. 'Neurotic' Americans and Europeans who had money and had escaped the trauma of war invested in the psychiatric treatments *de jour*. Their concerns were different than those of war victims. Psychodynamic theory different from Freud's flooded the scene. While intensive talk therapy was common to all, competing theories of the origins of commonly labeled mental aberrations of that time contributed much heat, but little light, to the practical issue of effective interventions to remediate more serious mental illness. For most psychiatric patients, institutional treatment remained just as barbaric as before the war. With rare exceptions, the average veteran with serious mental health concerns fared about the same following the Second World War as he had after the First World War.

And then there were the children. Autistic children at both ends of the spectrum were labeled with the term 'childhood psychosis'. Even when the term 'autism' was used, it was commonly conflated with 'childhood psychosis'. Misinformation regarding autism continued following Bruno Bettleheim's writings on autism in the mid 1950s. His writings regarding the reasons for autism were scientifically unsupported but considered 'holy writ' for decades by mental health professionals working with autistic children. Today, Bettleheim's theory on the cause of autism deserves the rejection it has received.

Although Asperger continued to remain active in the pediatric psychiatry field for three decades, his 1944 article was only 'discovered' by a team of English researchers in the early 1980s. In 1981, Lorna Wing coined the term 'Asperger Syndrome' (AS) after its discoverer. Despite hot debates between a handful of experts in argument about whether AS was a distinctly different phenomenon from Kanner's autism, Asperger's original article remained inaccessible to those who could not read German until its translation and re-publication in 1991 by Uta Frith. The article appeared as one of many in her edited collection of papers on Asperger Syndrome.

Definitional discussions raged throughout the 1980s. By the early 1990s there were no fewer than four competing sets of diagnostic criteria for AS. Most shared common features. Minor differences continued until the publication of criteria by the World Health Organization in the International Classification of Diseases (ICD-10, 1992) and the American Psychiatric Association's publication of its criteria in the Diagnostic Statistical Manual (DSM-IV, 1994). Debate concerning the validity and reliability of diagnostic criteria for Asperger Syndrome continues today. A revision of the DSM-IV, the DSM-IV-TR (2000) has been published. Discussion of the differences between high functioning autism (HFA) and Asperger Syndrome continues unabated. Perhaps by the projected publication date for the DSM-V (2005–2006), the debate will be settled.

So recent an official publication of the diagnostic criteria by the world's two leading medical organizations means that a vast majority of AS adults have never been formally diagnosed AS, but may have received a number of other diagnoses, all irritatingly off target.

Child specialists, educators, service providers and medical personnel still debate the authenticity of AS as a pervasive developmental condition. Many of them also debate the social wisdom of labeling children with the term. Autism is big business. Starting small in the early 1960s, 'we' now support an entire industry of medical and educational diagnosticians and treatment specialists. There's only one problem to this picture: the majority of autistic persons walking around are adults, not children.

It is a simple fact that few medical doctors understand AS. Most cannot diagnose it in adults. Adults who have been successfully medically diagnosed have usually turned to developmental pediatricians or psychiatrists familiar with the procedures used in diagnosing AS children and adolescents. Improved screening instruments continue to more accurately describe clusters of characteristics in children. Children are being diagnosed with AS at an earlier age. The best diagnostic practices affecting early identification of autistic children have pushed back the age for definitive diagnosis of AS in children into early pre-school years. Some promising instruments are in developmental stages for screening adults. Still, diagnosing children and adults with AS is a high art, not a science.

Children display the characteristics of AS quite openly. They have not yet learned adaptive behaviors, compensations or how to mask its effects. Unaided, few AS children develop successful strategies on their own to deal with all of its challenges. By the time adults seek a medical diagnosis, they have learned to suppress many of the outward manifestations of AS. The great cost of having done so is often the reason why adults seek a diagnosis in the first place. Many of their survival tools no longer work.

They find themselves under stress at work and in their personal lives. Often, persons who have AS remain misdiagnosed and treated for symptoms by specialists looking only at the symptoms and not the underlying reason for the symptoms. It may require considerable 'doctor shopping' to find a doctor competent and experienced with this condition who is able to see through the adaptive behaviors to confirm the existence of AS through the person's family accounts of childhood behavior and other past history. Where that information is not available, sensitive diagnosticians have begun to accept the patient's self-reports as sufficiently sound for the purpose of a definitive diagnosis. Professionals assuming this more enlightened approach believe that few persons who are not AS would seek out a diagnosis with such devastating implications.

Despite the explosion of information about Asperger Syndrome on the Internet and in printed media, one troubling issue related to the disorder is not often mentioned: the challenge of disclosure. Until recently, high-quality discussion has been missing about the effects of diagnosis on the individual and his or her family. Where a minor child is involved, parents and caretakers assume the role of educators for themselves and advocates to others for the child. Often, others are informed of the child's diagnosis before the child is told. Parents' decisions about how and when they inform their child are highly individual. There is no one-size-fits-all-situations guide for them to handle this difficult task. This process is a constant theme in support groups and Internet support groups and closed Email listservs.

Diagnosticians are still inexperienced or personally uncomfortable dealing with adult self-determination, disclosure and self-advocacy. Many diagnosticians have narrowed the scope of their practice just to diagnosis and evaluation. It is often up to other professionals to 'handle the other details', and when children are involved, other professionals often do. For adults professionally diagnosed with AS, the burden of revealing the diagnosis and offering further explanations to others falls on their own shoulders.

When dealing with you as an adult, the same professional may be far more comfortable discussing you and your issues with another professional. This is usually the case when you come for a diagnosis through a referral or request for a second opinion by another professional. If the diagnostician's report is required by an agency to substantiate your eligibility for a program, their information is frequently disbelieved, questioned, or rejected out of hand. This phenomenon is known as the 'Cassandra Syndrome'.

In the meantime, where does this leave you? What comes next?

Understanding your diagnosis, disclosing it to others and becoming an effective self-advocate comes next.

Your adult medical system may be set up so that diagnosticians don't have the time to discuss the next steps with you. It may be that they perceive themselves in their consultation role with you as authority figures and experts.

In fact, they may be, but this doesn't alter one very important fact. You have rights as an adult and as a patient that some diagnosticians are uncomfortable in recognizing. Once a diagnostician concludes that as an adult you have a 'condition' – and this includes any condition – your relationship to that professional undergoes a profound change.

Because a diagnostician is relating to you as an adult, he/she may assume that if you seek diagnosis, you should be capable of handling disclosure on your own. This may not be true. It is not unusual for a physician, after informing you of your diagnosis, to then to revert to his/her persona as just another intelligent, but uninformed adult who says to you: 'You are bright. You should be able to figure out the next steps on your own.'

Not so fast.

When you first consult with a diagnosing professional, you may not realize that you have started on your way to a major, life-changing event. The diagnostician is an important actor in *your* drama that has already begun to unfold. It is a drama with more than one scene and one act. In many instances once an adult, informed of his/her diagnosis, leaves a physician's office, both parties feel that is the end of their relationship.

Is it?

When I read report after report of this kind of scene in a diagnostician's office, I know, and the person telling me knows, that something has gone very wrong here. I suggest that the professional, already under obligation to 'do no harm', has an affirmative obligation before the consultation relationship with you is over. The professional has a moral responsibility to refer you to persons who can help you through the next steps.

The diagnostic and disclosure process

Experts in the field of such life-changing events such as cancer, neo-natal intensive care, natural and man-made disasters, emergency medicine, HIV/AIDS, Ebola virus, and other life-shattering and fatal occurrences, have developed a process to handle the patient, the family, and others affected by those events. Writers in the field of cognitive rehabilitation – which deals with traumatic brain injury, stroke, and other profound brain insults and developmental disorders – are careful to include their patients' whole environment to identify all the actors affected by this life-changing event. For their best advice to work, there must be a support network in place for their patient. If there isn't, they work very hard to build one.

There is one problem to this picture when it comes many late-diagnosed AS adults. Many AS adults do not have a similar support network.

If you believe you have AS, you may decide not to seek a formal diagnosis. This is really no one's business other than yours. Or is it? Let's assume a couple of things. If you are self-diagnosed, you have the same burden as medically diagnosed adults. When – not if – you disclose your AS to others, you are also faced with the additional difficulty of explaining your 'unofficial' diagnosis to others without 'the papers' to support your explanations. Regardless of how you come to your diagnosis, the process you go through getting it and dealing with it is the same.

Every AS person deals with diagnosis and disclosure issues in a unique way. If you are self-diagnosed, your diagnosis should be validated through the observations and comments of other adults with AS. This is called 'self-diagnosis, peer-confirmed'. Many self-diagnosed AS adults refrain from a formal diagnosis for as many valid reasons as there are individuals. If you have decided not to seek a formal diagnosis, I encourage you to write about your decision. You need not 'explain yourself' or justify yourself to anyone. This is your book. As with all of the questions posed in this chapter, my interest lies in helping you understand how you arrive at your own decisions.

If you seek a formal diagnosis, you should never do so to satisfy the needs of other people. Were you to do this, you really cannot represent only yourself in the diagnostic process. You are an adult. A good diagnostician should ask you about your own motivation and reasons for seeking a diagnosis, and determine whether you are there at the urging of other people. If you visit a diagnostician while riding astride another person's agenda, you may leave the professional's office with lingering doubt as to the wisdom of having sought official validation in the first place. This is one issue where others should never be permitted to determine your interests or run your life. In this one critical area, no other person has 'your interests' at heart. This is your issue, and yours alone.

The steps to diagnosis and disclosure

Here is an outline of the full process of diagnosis and disclosure. I arrived at this outline before reading any literature on the subject. The outline is derived from extensive discussions by AS adults on subscription Email lists not open to researchers or writers. As a participant in those forums, I have summarized the observations of at least 200 adults on the spectrum. There was remarkable similarity in the experiences described by each person, enough to convince me that this outline is valid. Its details are fleshed out following the outline.

The awakening

- Knowing that we are different;

- Hearing about HFA/AS;

- Curiosity;

- Self-informative research (all sources);

- Doubt or self-affirmation.

The diagnosis process:

- If through *self-diagnosis*, subjection to thorough self-evaluation, self-assessment, and history (history information often provided by others, principally family); determination of whether the self-diagnoser meets the criteria found in any of the four principal diagnostic criteria sources: Gillberg and Gillberg (1989); Szatmari, Bremner, and Nagy (1989); ICD-10 (1992); and DSM-IV (1994). Finally, acceptance by peers (similarly self-diagnosed or formally diagnosed by qualified and competent professionals);

- Seeking a *formal diagnosis* from an outsider (includes the process of identifying a knowledgeable diagnostician);

- The diagnostic consultation, and on some occasions, verbal statement of the diagnosis;

- The formal written diagnosis by the specialist, sometimes including recommendations for medication and support services;

- Depression starts to set in (often not noticeable);

- Return visit to referring physician, if any; otherwise, seeking out a support MD or psychological counselor;

- Discussion of the diagnosis; discussion and possible prescription of medication; discussion of and referrals to service providing specialists and/or support groups;

- Seeking of support from post-diagnostic process experts (medical social workers working in perinatal, neonatal, and infant intensive care wards; social workers, vocational rehabilitation counselors and peer counselors working in oncology, HIV, Intensive Care Units, Traumatic Brain Injury emergency and stroke wards and hospices, all experienced in personal loss and recovery work);

- Worsening of depression – sometimes still not noticeable to the person – which advances, sometimes, to a profound level possibly warranting crisis intervention;

- Other pre-existing or new medical conditions may kick in as the body reacts to increased stress.

Acceptance

- Disclosure to self;

- Application of labels given by others;

- Unfolding of the new identity and the simultaneous start of the personal grieving process;

- Shedding of the old self-identity;

- Mourning of the loss of the old identity;

- The beginning of the healing process;

- A sensation of the mind a-jumble.

Disclosure to the first person

- The dilemma of disclosure: whether to disclose; why disclose; whom to choose first; what to say; how to say it; when to disclose; how much; how fast; requests for confidentiality; affirmations of self-trust and dignity; creation and practise of the 'disclosure script' (all items in no particular order);

- The asking or not asking of others to assist in the disclosure process;

- The informed person's response (expect everything and everything. There are no rules here);

- The informed person's grieving process begins;

- The informed person's mourning process (discarding your old identification); formulating a personal definition of you; accepting your new identity as you express it);

- The informed person's healing;

- The beginning of a new relationship with the informed person.

You as a new person

- The challenge of introducing yourself to others (additional scripting, pre-testing and rehearsals);

- Your first introduction to another person;

- The compact on disclosure by others: rules for their disclosure of information about you;

- Moving on: informing the next person, and then the next;

- Variations on the same steps above for each new person, each new situation.

This description seems formal. At first glance, it appears too much, yet every adult with high functioning autism or Asperger Syndrome takes each step to one degree or another. Because of the absence of others smoothing the path for an adult who must do this on his/her own, certain of the stages can appear almost arrested or delayed, but they do occur at the person's own pace.

Notice that none of the steps mention independence, distinguish between degrees of sociability, or compare the AS person with any others, AS or otherwise. For each individual newly diagnosed with AS, the first steps taken down the path are lonely ones.

Discussion

When you discuss HFA/AS with persons having bad information about autism, your experience is often more challenging than dealing with people who have no knowledge at all. This is true for those who profess expertise in fields such as education, rehabilitation, general counseling, and employment counseling.

Mature adults seeking advice from such 'experts' frequently encounter full-blown general social prejudice and ignorance about hidden disabilities. Despite what they may have recently read or heard, many professionals are slow to alter their original thinking about pervasive developmental disorders. Many are trapped by the dead hand of four generations of psychodynamic theory.

Despite their knowledge of drugs targeted to affect specific areas or functions in the brain and thus certain behaviors, many of these same professionals doggedly maintain that HFA and AS are not really neuro-biologically based. Blaming us for our manifestations and trying useless talk therapy or powerful broadband drugs is a common 'expert' approach taken by many professionals when they work with AS children and adults. Often, we are regarded as willful and defiant, untrusting, mildly schizophrenic or borderline personality, obsessive compulsive, and inevitably too 'old' or 'beyond help' and thus ineligible for assistance.

In addition to these sentiments, we encounter attitudes such as 'Since you have done OK in the past, you do not need help now'. If help is offered, it is often extended in such a way as to keep us less visible to the public, and to 'protect' us from mainstream society. Faced with this attitude, we have begun to wonder just who is being protected. Many experts stand as gatekeepers to the benefits of adult society. It is precisely in the middle of the river dividing 'us' from 'them' that the issues of our adult independence, integrity, competence and employment, stand as islands. Somehow, just our *being* there worries experts about how the stream flows. Our struggle is not only about independence; it is also about acceptance and inclusion.

This unenlightened attitude is thousands of years old. It comes from many helping professionals convinced that they know what is best for us and so can speak authoritatively on our behalf. When challenged for this behavior, experts often sigh and say that social attitudes are not likely to change quickly, and that as a disabled person they expect us to perform at our lowest level well. Whole systems and institutions are designed around this attitude. Its effect is to foster our continued dependency. For years, it also stood at the foundation of social work. That is no longer the case, but it is still widely expressed in actual practise, despite changes in the language of public policies.

Disclosure to family, relatives, friends or acquaintances is fraught with danger. Anxiety escalates when informing others outside our support system. Deciding what to reveal and how to do it is as troublesome as deciding who to tell. 'Why' and 'when' are often just as difficult. By the time we consider disclosure, we may be very well informed about AS. This is a blessing as well as a curse. We can be our own best advocates. Unfortunately, due to excessive enthusiasm, poor timing or bad judgment we can also be our own worst enemies and saboteurs.

After receiving a formal diagnosis of adult AS, most of us go through a period of depression. The length and severity of this depression varies widely. Few diagnosticians prepare us for this because the diagnostic visit might the only time they see us. Most people are unaware of the aftereffect of this diagnosis. From what is known from parents' reactions of shock and depression following their AS child's diagnosis, it is surprising that more has not been said about post-diagnostic depression in independent adults. Some parents with children diagnosed with AS are also on the spectrum themselves. That diagnosticians rarely take this commonly-known information to heart when informing them of a child's diagnosis is shocking and inexcusable.

Most parents writing about their child's recent diagnosis report how unprepared they were for their own reaction. Many report being devastated by the news. Parent support groups, newsgroups and Internet Email lists are valuable to parents going through this experience. Joining similar adult on-line newsgroups and listservs is of equal value to newly diagnosed AS adults.

Following diagnosis, some of us may show great caution about how much we reveal to others, how we say it, and how we expect the information to be received. Often, the persons closest to us require some time in accepting our information and showing an understanding of what we say. Up to the time we inform them, they have thought of us in a certain way. What we may now expect from them is to think of us differently. Asking them to do that means they must put away their old thoughts and mourn our old identity. Our own depression involves the same kind of mourning because until the recent past, we thought of ourselves as a different person too.

When we tell others of our AS, they may have an 'AHA!' experience. There is an equal chance that their understanding will be like the gradual dawning of the light. If we flood them with a blaze of information, they cannot really hear what we say. They are in shock. Like people subjected to bright lights and loud sounds, they may protect their eyes and ears, just be stunned, or withdraw. There are other people, often very close to us, who just do not understand. They may never understand. With everyone we tell, it is better for us to know in advance that we should expect *any* kind of reaction, not just the one we hope for.

Disclosure and the workplace

The personal work we first do regarding disclosure to family and friends prepares us to explore these issues with employment professionals. By understanding how we handle this issue with family and acquaintances, we can help professionals design safe and effective methods to guide us through the same minefield at work.

Many employment counselors are not comfortable with the idea that persons with disabilities are entitled to equal consideration for competitive employment (real, market-rate work). Some of us may not be ready for that kind of work either, but that is ultimately our decision to make, not theirs. Persons uncomfortable with the idea of full employment for persons with disabilities are bearers of 80 years of old-style vocational rehabilitation thinking. That way of thinking can't be reversed overnight, but there are things we can do to make sure we aren't saddled with 'their' problem. One way is to be vigilant yet realistic about our employment counseling experiences. When we first face knowledge about our AS, we may not appreciate the ramifications of that knowledge once we put it into the hands of others. If we do a good job of understanding the relationship between our 'brand' of AS with our interest in work, we are better prepared to deal with counselor misunderstanding, misperception, and outright resistance to our ideas.

Understanding ourselves as workers is what this book is all about.

No one said understanding us is easy. Double that for expecting others to understand us.

Employment counseling professionals may be in conflict about how to discuss the issue of disclosing our diagnosis to an employer, our co-workers, or other service providers. There are many reasons for their discomfort. When we enter into a counseling relationship with them, one of their jobs is to explore our concerns about disclosure. It is also their job to listen to our concerns first before sharing their own concerns. The way they treat this topic may have nothing to do with our interests and everything to do with the 'politics' of how they deal with employers and other professionals. A good employment counselor should not make our success in disclosing at the workplace dependent on their new or continued relationship with an employer. However, many do, and we should be wise to this political factor in their 'system' as they work with us.

Discrimination, disclosure and employment law

Protections accorded workers with disabilities vary across jurisdictions and between cultures. The author is most familiar with employment and disability practices in the United States, so some of what appears in this book may not apply to your condition. Knowing our AS proclivity to 'adhere to the rules,' let me warn you that from this point on, nothing I say should be considered as legal advice or as a substitute for good, local information applicable to the employment conditions where you live and work. In this section I refer not to 'us' but to you, the reader. Blanket statements for all of us are inappropriate when it comes to the matters to be discussed below.

Until recently, disabled workers were not protected against discrimination due to their disabilities in the workplace. Starting in the early 1970s in the United States, the Vocational Rehabilitation Act of 1973 contained provisions designed to protect students and employees in government and in public and private business from discrimination. Section 504 of the Act works best with public sector discrimination. Although the law was passed in 1973, it took years for the Nixon, Ford, and Carter administrations to begin writing implementing regulations interpreting the law. It was clear to everyone concerned about the employment and other interests of disabled people that something more needed to be done. Once regulations were written, their weakness in applying to the private sector finally convinced disabled activists and a shamed US Congress to pass the Americans with Disabilities Act (ADA) of 1990. Following passage of the federal Act, many states enacted mini-ADA laws of their own.

Success in enforcement has been mixed. It took another Republican administration two years to write the first implementing regulations for the ADA, regulations mainly concerned with accessibility issues and architectural barriers. Progress in the broader area of employment discrimination has been slow and subject to the fits and starts of the US federal judicial system. Unlike the accessibility and barriers issues addressed in the first round of regulations, disability employment discrimination issues require attention in individual court cases to 'make law'. Those cases gradually percolated up through the appellate ladder to reach their first definitive national interpretation late in the 1990s. The US Supreme court was petitioned earlier to hear several cases but declined until a sufficient number of cases were at mid-level in the judicial system to warrant attention at the highest level.

In the spring of 1999, the US Supreme Court issued a handful of employee discrimination opinions designed to provide some guidance to the lower courts and employers involved in ADA legal complaints. The results were mixed. Many disability employment attorneys and advocates feel that this first batch of cases accepted by the Supreme Court contained bad cases to begin with. Thus, they made for 'bad law'. Other commentators suggest that even bad cases make good law on occasion, and look forward to additional cases to even out the record.

At the date of this book's writing, several federal intermediate courts, the US Circuit Courts of Appeal, have ruled that one or both acts of Congress referred to above do not apply to the states in their circuit. Other circuit courts believe that they do. This conflict of law must be resolved at the highest level. The US Supreme Court, mindful of this present muddle wherein the law extends to workers only in parts of the country, appears to be in no hurry to resolve this conundrum. Readers anxious to get a clear picture of the legal status of protection against employer discrimination must wait along with everyone else for matters to be settled. Because disability employment law is built case by case, it is likely that 'the law' will remain unsettled for some time.

Even with matters as apparently unsettled as they are, a number of things can be said about the principles and politics behind discrimination and disclosure. An entire sub-specialization in employment law has developed to deal with disability issues. Many complaints are handled through the mediation process, resulting in settlements that allow the employee to leave an uncomfortable or discriminatory situation with the means for support in the form of a substantial cash award.

Once things get to the point of filing a formal complaint, the reality is that the disabled employee will be very unlikely to be able to stay on with that employer. If the employee does stay, there may be transfers, dead-end assignments and further recrimination ahead. Retaliation following a 'win' is often just as difficult to prove as the original discrimination. For the first-time victor, the second time around the track may prove expensive, time consuming, and of little real value. By the time a second suit is filed, good will between the parties has been exhausted. This is why most attorneys recommend that with the first settlement, the client ' take the money and run'. Legally, the employee could again try the same complaint and suit process. In practice, they have ruined their future with that employer by having 'gone formal' in the first place.

These are important considerations to weigh in determining how you wish to raise any issue of your AS with an employer, whether it is a prospective or current one. If you are presently a client of vocational rehabilitation, the fact that you are disabled has proceeded you in the employment path. Depending on the agency you may be working with, details of your AS may or may not have been disclosed. Ideally, you should have been in charge of the entire process. In reality, things are never quite that clean.

If you are seeing a private counselor, you should be in total control of any information regarding disclosure of your AS. Counselors at all levels are bound by the codes of ethics of their professions to observe the confidentiality and privacy concerns of their clients. Any violation of these standards usually guarantees swift punishment, and may result in suspension or loss of their license or privilege to practice.

As a matter of law – now in question in some jurisdictions in the US – employers are prohibited from asking a job applicant whether the he or she is disabled. Even if the ADA hadn't been passed in 1990, and gone into effect in 1992, employer attorneys now routinely advise employers not to ask. To a certain extent, this same prohibition is attached to the employers' relations with an employee already hired, but the rules change a bit. If you engage in conduct resulting in discipline, the employer is entitled to ask you whether there is anything in your personal life or otherwise which may have led to the incident or behavior which has provoked disciplinary action. If you answer in the negative, the employer is left to draw his/her own conclusions about your fitness for the job. Repeated incidents without further explanation on your part can lead to a record justifying more disciplinary action, including your termination. If you endanger yourself or others by something you do or fail to do, the employer may ask you further questions, including questions relating to medications you may be taking. Under other circumstances an employer can ask you to disclose this information if medication is obviously affecting your performance in an adverse manner. The key words are 'obviously' and 'performance' – both matters subject to objective examination following a formal investigation. While the investigation must proceed according to guidelines, the employer conducts it. As you can imagine, outcomes may vary.

By the time anything at work has prompted the attention of your employer, your fellow employees are no doubt aware of something. The reason for your being questioned by an employer may involve concerns shared with your employer by a fellow worker. If the employer is sensitive, the matter can be handled discretely, but the situation may require closure with the fellow employee who reported something amiss. How your employer accomplishes that with the other employee is the employer's business, not yours.

When you apply for a job and have a condition that you know will affect your performance or ability to undertake essential tasks and duties of the job, you are obliged to inform your prospective employer about this. If you fail to do so, you cannot later raise the issue of your disability in order to receive any of the legal protections accorded you as a disabled person. Telling an employer that you cannot do certain things, or have limitations, is not necessarily a tip-off about your disability. You may not have the skills or training, neither of which may have anything do with your AS.

Many people cannot perform all the duties of a job, but are hired anyway. Their other strengths and assets outweigh whatever limitations they may have with respect to some tasks. Usually, an employer will come to some agreement with the employee about either delegating the tasks or modifying the job description. In any event, the employer wants you badly enough to do this. One fact to keep in mind is this: the employer is not obligated to do anything until and unless there is an offer for hire, and you accept it. You are then in a position to negotiate such arrangements.

Some of us are rather righteous about what we consider the duties and obligations of others to accommodate us. If you approach an employer with the attitude that you have a right to a position, and you say something to that effect, you will not get further than your demand. I use the term 'demand' deliberately. Even in a market favorable to workers, no employer will hire someone with such an attitude. Going into a hiring situation where you either quote the law or your understanding of it at the beginning of the application process also equals 'no job'.

I must be direct in mentioning this because many persons with Asperger Syndrome engage in all-or-nothing thinking. Much private discussion between persons with AS reveals a rigidity and moralism that is simply unacceptable in the hiring situation. Some AS adults have horrible histories of part-time work, no work, 'attitude' problems at work, and myriad other reasons for new employers not to consider hiring them. These same histories can work against a person lucky enough to make it past the interviewer and onto the payroll. The first rule for everyone with a tendency to think and act this way is to stop. Thinking this way leads to behavior that is contrary to your survival as a worker. That some of us engage in it, seeming unable to control it, is a problem for *us* to work on, not someone else.

By the time you have written your biography chapters in this workbook, you will have a lot of self-knowledge at your fingertips. You know much about what has worked for you and what hasn't. You will know about specific learning and performance areas you need to address to make a difference in your present or future work. This knowledge can make you a good self-advocate. As with other kinds of knowledge, how you choose to use it to your advantage requires good judgment, perspective, and your use of a specialized kind of common sense.

One thing we know about ourselves is that we do have weakness in these areas. But weakness does not mean an absence of those elements. The disclosure and advocacy questions in Part 3 of this workbook deal with the following items:

- Who
- When
- How
- What
- Why.

Tricks of the trade – practical tips on self-advocacy

We'll go right down the list. Handling every single one of them will require that you rehearse your responses with someone you trust. You can rehearse the challenges you might find with each of these items, so that when the time comes, you should be fully prepared and in charge of your own process of self-advocacy.

Who

Autism is not something that most people understand. High functioning autism, or AS, is something that fewer people understand. Telling everyone about your Asperger Syndrome will leave a lot of folks confused, often wondering why you bothered to tell them in the first place. Ask yourself what is to be accomplished by telling any person you consider informing about your AS. We had a reputation as children, and many of us as adults, of being 'little professors'. Now we're grown-up 'professors'. Most people don't relate to pedantic persons, and we can be pedantic. Choose your 'who' wisely. A general rule of thumb is that whoever you tell you must trust, and second, that their knowledge about you will do you no harm, and, of equal importance, do them no harm. For some people, telling them about AS is like throwing a dead fish at them. They don't know what to do with the information, and that can make them dangerous to you. Be careful.

With someone you trust, tell them as much as you can about the 'who' person. Ask your trusted person to play-act the role of the 'who' person, and then you can practice interacting with that 'who' person through role-playing. Have your trusted person throw you some tough questions, things you know that the real 'who' is likely to ask. Have them do some of the same things, and practice dealing with that behavior.

Rehearse.

When

This is a toughie. We are known to be impulsive and impatient. We often interrupt other people with our business, paying little attention to what they are doing at that moment. Many of us are clueless about these matters, yet this is one issue where timing is crucial. If you must tell someone, make sure they have the time to listen, and you have the time to do it right. If that person is busy, make an appointment. They will appreciate your consideration because it shows you respect the other things they have to do. Even if you have an appointment, you might want to remind them of the appointment shortly beforehand, and when arriving, check in with them to find out whether they still have time to talk. If they don't, and they tell you that, reschedule.

'When' also means when *you* are ready. For this issue, you must take charge of your own time. If you are not ready to discuss or disclose and someone asks you to do so, your wish to satisfy him or her may be very dangerous to your survival on the job. You may say things you do not mean. You may say too much, or commit other kinds of mistakes that leave a lasting impression. All of this may happen because you did not take charge of your own time.

If you are concerned that this might happen, have someone practice interrupting you when you are doing something else, and have him or her demand that you answer his or her questions. Rehearse how to be polite and control these events. Develop and memorize scripts that allow you to escape the demand and the pressure and still be polite, but in charge. To rehearse for this, you might want to practice telling someone a secret that isn't so loaded with importance. Practicing this way will teach you how to handle these disruptions safely. Once you have done that, you can move on to rehearsing your disclosure.

How

Remember that people learn in different ways. The way you learn things may be quite different than how another person learns, and the trick to mastering 'how' is to know how that person learns best. The following suggestion may sound ludicrous, but try it. If you know who you wish to disclose your AS to, approach them when they seem open to being approached, and ask them how they learn about something completely unconnected with what you want to tell them. If they have an interest or a skill, ask them outright how they learnt that skill. Ask them about one other unrelated matter, and then sneak around to the topic of how they learn new things about other people. That's a harmless enough question, and they will probably want to tell you. Listen carefully to what they say. They are telling you about their 'learning hooks', and it is those hooks you want to engage when you are ready to disclose your AS to them.

Before you tell them, rehearse.

What

We get into trouble with this one all the time. Many of us can't seem to stop once we get going. We know that, yet we forge ahead anyhow, hoping the other person will put up with it.

Don't be so sure. Not with this topic. Remember, the topic is you, not just AS. We may think we are interesting topics all by ourselves. That may be true, but that's not the point. Other people may not think so. Your point in disclosing your AS is to provide just enough information for people to understand your particular job challenges. They don't want to see or hear about the contents of the whole kitchen sink.

Brevity. The best rule is to say as little as you can in as few words as possible, and keep those words simple and focused on your exact workplace challenges. Anything more and you will have their eyelids fluttering and boredom setting in. What you say to anyone at work about your AS should be directly related to the other five basic questions listed above. Tell them something in order to explain yourself or start negotiations. Do not chatter on. Your particular 'medical' condition is of little interest to people otherwise. Try to keep that in mind.

Rehearse what you are going to say with a trusted person. What you say may depend on why, who, when, how, and how much you need to say. One thing to keep uppermost in your mind during your rehearsals with a trusted person is that you are providing this information for a practical purpose. You want to get something from having said it. AS may be fascinating to you. It may even be fascinating to the other person. However, they only need the information that will allow you to keep doing your job. The best way to guarantee that you don't say too much is to rehearse saying your short piece. When you master the technique, say your short piece to the important person and stop. Just like that. It's harder than you think.

Rehearse.

Why

This is the mother lode. You know about your AS. You know whom you are going to tell. You've got the timing down right. You know how the other person learns, and you've tuned your information to the way they learn about people. You know what to say, and not a word more. So, why? Why tell?

There is no limit to the number of reasons why you should disclose. Remember, at the heart of a 'why' is 'whether' you should tell at all. Has something happened at work that is best covered with an explanation? Think first whether your telling will 'fix' what needs to be fixed. If all the person has at the end of your disclosure is an interesting story and no way to recoup a loss or fix something (including a relationship) that is broken, rethink the whole process. People communicate for a reason. In my case, I had to plead my way into being retained by explaining that I couldn't function in a more complex job. It was either the dumbed down job or out the door. I couldn't afford the second choice.

Frankly, that was, and still is a terrible reason to disclose, but it was all I had at the time. My disclosure happened after I had just been diagnosed. I didn't know there were guidelines that would have made it easier. I was out there on my own, not realizing that, when I disclosed, I was very vulnerable. I was at the bottom of a profound reactive trough of depression following my diagnosis.

Another 'why' issue: Is it worthwhile to disclose? Are you so close to quitting the job that telling wouldn't make any difference? If you are at the beginning of a new job and know you can handle its challenges, why throw a monkey wrench into the deal? Check the situation out carefully. Will disclosing your AS increase your chance of getting what you need by disclosing? There is a difference between hope and reality. If you can't think straight about this question, don't even think of disclosing. You aren't sufficiently prepared to try. Unlike other things you do, disclosure can't be undone. It can't be re-tried in an effort to make the effort come out better.

Disclosure is a one-chance affair. I don't say this because I'm paranoid. I'm not. It just happens to be the truth. Ask any rehabilitation counselor whose client has 'blown it' with a prospective or actual employer. Ask any mental health professional whose patient, despite the best counseling, went ahead and showed bad judgment against the counselor's advice. Ask any professional whose disclosure has damaged a client. You won't find one who hasn't had that experience. It's a part of life, and a very painful one at that. They learn how to avoid it happening again, but the experience remains indelibly etched in their memory.

My experience taught me something. After the fact, it taught me the value of each of the five points of this section. It also taught me that the situation is different for every person, and that there are no one-size-fits-all approaches to this dilemma. Some of us are perfectly capable of taking the knowledge, going through the phases of self-determination, diagnosis, and the aftermath, and emerging relatively unscathed in one, new piece at the other end. Others of us are very vulnerable and very hurt to begin with, and we need time and understanding just to get a grip on ourselves. This is a solo act, but like learning to ride a bicycle it helps when others get us started. All of us would benefit from the help of others to pace us through this personal process.

Buying help

You now are aware of the bare minimum requirements for making a safe disclosure. It is up to you to exercise your best judgment, including soliciting the advice of a trusted person to help you do that. All of us need a trusted person to rehearse disclosure. No matter how much we think we 'have it together', there will be things another person can observe about us that tells them otherwise. It is better they tell us in a safe environment than our finding out about it after we have hurt ourselves in the real test. Some of us are so isolated that we can't easily identify such a person. That's the time to think of 'buying' one in the person of a professional counselor, employment specialist, and coach or job developer.

If you are enrolled with vocational rehabilitation, request training to help you disclose in a safe, controlled way. By this time, you know enough about your AS to know your points of vulnerability and where your 'AS-ness' has worked against you. You have identified an area where training would have a beneficial, employment related outcome. The purpose of vocational rehabilitation, at least in the US, is to provide disabled persons with the tools to attain and retain employment. They have a budget for training. 'Buy' a trainer.

You can also 'buy' training if you are a student in public school special education in the US and are age 16 or older. Federal special education law encourages you to participate in your transition program. That law affects every school district in the country. When you reach the age of 16, your public school system is responsible for setting up your transition team. The purpose of the team is to address needs you will have after you finish high school. Under the law, you may request services and training unrelated to merely completing your high school program. A transition plan is geared towards assuring your success as an independent adult. Disclosure skills will be essential for you to have in higher education, vocational training, community college, the work force or any other place you see yourself once you finish with school. Under current law, your state vocational rehabilitation agency is a mandated partner in your transition team. They may or may not agree to pay for such training while you are still in school, but they are required to share resources with your school district. Every state vocational rehabilitation agency now has contracts with the state department of education setting up collaboration arrangements with local school districts. You need not worry who pays for the training. It's up to your school to figure that out.

However, it's up to you to ask for it. Start asking for it now, and don't stop until you get it. Vocational rehabilitation and special education are systems. Learn to 'play the system'.

Workplace accommodations

Despite our diagnosis, most of us think of ourselves as able, but with some challenges. Many of us are too embarrassed to ask for accommodation as disabled persons. We have been shamed into thinking we have no right to special treatment. You may not even need to ask. As a matter of practice, if you've worked for some time you may actually have some 'hidden' accommodations already working for you. Many of them are informal and unstated. They are accommodations nonetheless.

For some of us, our challenges are more severe, but they may be handled through accommodation. If we wish to exercise our option under the law, there are formal requirements that involve notifying the employer and providing medical documentation if requested. Under American disability law there may be other criteria to be met for you can negotiate a reasonable accommodation with your employer. Unless you work in a government agency or a non-profit organization with funding from the government, I advise you to exercise caution in formally invoking the ADA and when rebuffed, turning immediately to thoughts of a lawsuit. Although you may get what you need, to twist the words of old popular song, 'you may not get want you want'. Personal accommodations won by an adversarial process are rarely long lasting or satisfactory.

Much of what you can secure as an accommodation for some of your AS challenges is dependent upon your skill as a negotiator. If you've been a successful self-advocate in the past even before you were diagnosed with AS, you might already have successfully negotiated accommodations. Employers often build accommodations into their workplace. Ready-made accommodations may include a policy allowing for flextime work, self-selection of work partners and certain work conditions, and provisions for privacy and freedom from distraction. To avoid favoritism and creation of cliques, employers may direct the membership of work groups or designate work partners. They may offer generous personal leave, compensatory time, work-from-home options, as well as good personnel practices such as a good health plan allowing for psychological counseling. Many employers also have employee assistance programs (EAPs), special services available to employees with family or personal problems or problems directly related to work challenges. These accommodations are often part of a package of benefits available to all workers whether they are disabled or not. You might be able to trade one of your special skills or talents to access accommodations ordinarily not available to workers at your level of employment. This kind of 'horse trading' happens all the time, although it is not publicized. Informal use of some workplace privileges is a well-kept secret.

Many employers recognize the value of relatively low cost assistive technology and ergonomically designed tools and workspaces. In the long run, these 'tools' save the employer money. Others allow employees to work at home or in unconventional locations due to temporary family emergencies. Others allow employees to trade hours or jobs, all in the interest of having a cross-trained, well-prepared workforce. Still others encourage employees to take classes for personal or work-related self-improvement, and make tuition or other in-kind assistance available.

The point to this short review of accommodations is to show you that an accommodation you negotiate could be of benefit to employees other than yourself. The most successful accommodations are ones that employers can leave in place after you leave, thus making them available to other employees. These accommodations then become a part of the entire workplace culture. Here is why: it's a matter of dollars and cents. If they develop an accommodation unique to you, with no universality to it, they may become reluctant to hire additional employees who require completely different, highly individuated arrangements. It really doesn't matter what the disability laws say. Employers have to run their businesses, and their disability law compliance plans are costs they figure into their overhead.

Employers are getting better about thinking of their employees as individuals first, and special expenses second. Nevertheless, we have a long way to go. Even though the term 'reasonable accommodation' in American disability law refers to an arrangement made for an individual person, the best accommodations approach being 'person-neutral' and flexible enough that with minimum tinkering, others can avail themselves of them after you leave. In your approach to negotiating an accommodation, keep such considerations in mind.

Try to think of an arrangement that can benefit other employees even while you are there. Employers like these kinds of arrangements. They don't even have to come up with them on their own. Swallow your pride and allow your employer to take full credit in public for what you crafted in private. Community recognition and respect means a lot to them. Except for a small nick to your ego, this kind of an accommodation is exactly the kind of 'win–win' settlement that keeps relationships in the workforce in a positive mode.

If you come up with innovations that allow you to learn a job or its tasks easier, you may not be the only worker to benefit from this development. If your workplace is one that encourages cost-savings and honors employees' suggestions, what works for you may very well be recognized as a benefit to others. If this happens, prepare to be recognized for your contribution. (If you have difficulty accepting praise, now is the time to consider working on *that* challenge with someone you trust.)

If a low-tech solution to your challenge is available, choose it every time. Negotiation generally works best when both parties are satisfied with the outcome. Neither side gets all it wants. Avoid 'holding out on principle' or going for an ideal or perfect solution. For example, repositioning lighting, closing a door, wearing hearing protection and other sensory protective safety devices, using a different chair, securing permission to take breaks other than at regular times are all possible low tech accommodations made at minimal cost to your employer. Such improvements can also lower the employer's insurance premiums as well. Helping an employer reduce his exposure to liability at the same time employee productivity is increased is a win–win proposition. You can negotiate accommodations that allow you to do what you can do better. Your employer then makes his money from your increased productivity.

There are some accommodations not so as easy to negotiate, but possible nonetheless. These are the ones that allow you to avoid tasks you can't perform, or perform only with great difficulty, time, and cost to the employer. Negotiating for these accommodations involves the same skill as playing some card games. Many of us dislike games because the rules seem so arbitrary and make little sense. This is one game where the rules, silly as they may seem to you, are essential for your survival, retention, and advancement in the workplace. Just like basic dress and self-care conventions imposed on all workers, you must observe them to keep your spot in the workforce.

Think of the game analogy for a moment longer. You can offer to 'sweeten the pot' with a contribution of a talent or skill that isn't a part of your job description but that may be valuable to the employer anyway. Perhaps you can trade that asset for a task for your job the employer is willing to delegate to another worker, or to another job. The only caution I'd advise is in giving too much in trade for a minor item. Avoid the temptation to offer to do anything just to have an unpleasant task traded away. Like anyone else, employers love a bargain. They can take advantage of people, although things don't usually start out that way.

Employers respect persons who have a good sense of their self-worth. By being too free with things unrelated to the reasons you were hired, you set yourself up for possible abuse. If you feel uncomfortable about the equities of a 'trade', you are probably pushing your own tolerance envelope. Honor your discomfort, and hold onto your assets for the next round. If the employer finds you too agreeable to a bad deal, when times are tough you might find yourself having agreed to be the first out the door during a layoff or downsizing.

Once you start your negotiations, if things start to get uncomfortable, say so. Request a time out, or say that you are feeling uncomfortable about the direction the conversation is taking. You would like some time to think about what has been said. A surprising thing may happen. You might discover your employer is just as uncomfortable as you are. Your request for time out provides both of you an opportunity to step back and assess your positions. You can agree to meet later on the issue. This is an honest, respectable way to handle discomfort. Your employer will respect you even more for being able to monitor your comfort level and handle the situation in a responsible manner.

In your quest for accommodation, think of others who could be your allies in making the bid. You might have fellow workers who agree with your ideas, but are afraid to make a suggestion themselves. For them, the change would be a convenience. For you, it is a necessity. If you feel they would benefit from an accommodation you personally ask for, check the strength of their support by asking them whether they could raise their hands if your accommodation came up for a public show of hands. If you sense any resistance, you now realize how personal your quest really is. This will give you a sense of perspective. It will also give you a chance to consider other accommodations that gain greater support from your fellow workers. You may not have the allies or the personal strength to fight for a particular accommodation at this time. There is always later.

You've maybe heard of the expression 'Pick your battles wisely'. Negotiating over accommodations is when that expression really means something. There is always another time and another opportunity to revisit the subject. Go into negotiations prepared to give as well as take. Through all of this, you are learning to become a skilled office politician. That's hardly a role you thought of when you requested an accommodation.

It is a respected role. Be proud of it.

CHAPTER 3

Social Skills

The brain and learning social skills

There is a growing body of literature written by psychologists, educational figures and medical specialists with good knowledge of AS. I do not discount the value of this research. This book couldn't have been written without it. Most research on AS behavior involves medically diagnosed individuals and is informed by a traditional medical model. A medical model is a model built around pathology and disease. Until recently, it was thought that once an individual reached a certain level of maturity, little more could be done to 'retrain' the brain and, by extension, redirect adult human thinking and behavior.

Even before Decade of the Brain studies showed the brain to be infinitely more complex than once thought, psychologists developed cognitive therapy as a way of working with high functioning clients whose behavior and thought patterns were unaffected by traditional talk therapy. Elements of cognitive therapy are now accepted in the field of adult cognitive rehabilitation. Some AS adults report that cognitive-behavioral therapy works for them. There is growing anecdotal evidence that this type of therapy may be effective for adults with AS.

Current rehabilitation work with traumatic brain injury, adult stroke, and individuals with lifelong cognitive deficits has capitalized on new knowledge of the integrative features of brain functioning. Lost communication and organizational skills can be restored. Head injury accident victims and victims of non-geriatric adult stroke can re-learn language and social skills through careful, methodical training in rehabilitation. Functional Magnetic Resonance Imaging research of the brain in action shows that many persons with these conditions share brain electrical activity patterns similar to those of individuals with autism. Medical researchers are hesitant to draw broad conclusions from small, exploratory research efforts. Functional imaging research for adults with autism has just begun. If new neural pathways can be constructed to re-establish executive function loss in persons with traumatic brain injury or stroke, there might be a way to construct pathways for language pragmatics and executive functions in the brains of persons who never had them in the first place. That sounds like us.

Recent brain bank studies conducted in the field of Alzheimer disease suggests that the brains of the very old (people over 80 years of age) appear to generate new cells at the lowest level of the brain identified with primitive memory and basic emotions. Memory is intimately allied with learning and the executive functions of the brain. If these findings are verified through additional studies, they will put an end to any argument about whether mature adults are capable of learning functions once thought impossible for them. As of the date of this writing, not much research has been done with AS adults to determine whether rehabilitation and remedial therapies known to be effective with these other individuals can have a similar effect with us. Until recently, money available for research has been directed towards ever increasing knowledge about the brain and the human genome. There are calls for practical brain research studies with adults, but the spotlight for medical research shifts focus very slowly.

Even with evidence that adults learn throughout our lifetime, there is good reason why all experts recommend early intensive childhood intervention for children identified as autistic. It works. Until very recently, educational research on AS was heavily influenced by older assumptions that brains of older children are incapable of meaningful development. Current research suggests that there are two growth spurt periods of the brain. One is for the well-recognized period of childhood extending to early adolescence. Another has been identified as occurring in late adolescence and early adulthood.

As children age and learning demands become more complex, most educators still believe that once a student reaches a certain age, from the school's point of view, efficient learning can no longer take place. These are policy decisions unsupported by current science. Administrators discuss learning probabilities in the language of 'cost benefits analysis' using the formulae of accountants. To a certain extent, administrators must think this way. They must allocate finite special education resources efficiently. There is only one problem with such thinking. Autistic children are not 'efficient' learners. Many autistic children learn everything in fits and starts. They are most inefficient in learning social skills. So are autistic adults.

Fortunately, experts in adult education have recognized the implications of current brain research. They are far more open than their K-12 colleagues to the idea of continued learning of new skills by adults with vastly different cultural backgrounds and educational experiences.

In the United States, many educators' positive vision of what adults can learn is opposed by a medical and vocational rehabilitation model that focuses on disability and pathology, not ability and wellness. That model is reinforced by private insurance industry practices that support only minimal cognitive remediation. Insurance industry policies are governed by market-capitalism's 'bottom-line thinking.' The medical and the insurance industries exert a major influence on the American national and state legislatures. For us, cognitive remediation is a term we can identify with training in social skills. Until political money flows in streams favorable to adult capabilities, enterprising adults interested in pushing ahead in their own training are forced by the system to 'go it alone'.

Since high functioning autism is not widely understood by either adult educators or most professional psychologists working with adults, their expectations about our capacity to change remains low. They tend to see the global challenges we face as insurmountable without taking the time to determine what particular areas of our life we would like to work on. They are also distressed by how slowly we change. Much of their counsel is for us to accept ourselves as we are. If our lives aren't working well, few of us are satisfied with such advice. We know there is more to life than resignation. We do many things that we would like to change. We want to be in charge of making that choice. A principal purpose of this workbook is to help you identify areas where you feel change is needed, and to move towards that change at a rate you can deal with.

Communication and social skills

The learning of language and social skills is vital for successful adult life. According to experts who track the effect of early learning of social skills, neurotypical children have the majority of basic social skills in place by the time they are four years old. Neurotypical children learn many of these skills early and by a process of osmosis and intuition. Autistic children do not. A number of characteristic features of AS explain this difference.

The learning of language involves the integration of multisensory experience (reception), effective mental processing, and appropriate expression. Persons diagnosed with AS have varying degrees of sensory deficit or hypersensitivities that have an impact on our social behavior. The unevenness of childhood development left some of us with developmentally delayed speech, while others of us demonstrated linguistic precocity. In many instances, we used words with an inadequate understanding of their full meaning (language pragmatics).

Most of us with our advanced vocabularies and precocious reading skills (hyperlexia) preferred the company of adults, but this very preference cut us off from learning and testing out language and behavior appropriate for our age peers. We learned how to charm adults with our erudition. For those of us who chose to avoid involvement with adults or children, we became shy and/or aloof.

What many of us didn't learn were the basic 'vocabulary words' of social communication, the building blocks of learning not merely how to get along with other children, but also how to survive as unsupported, independent adults. No wonder parents of AS children are berated for being overprotective. Until their children learn basic social skills, they need to be shielded. The major question for most parents of AS children is how and when to withdraw their protection.

Play and recreation

Seeking out the company of adults, or avoiding people altogether is common for persons with AS. With both behaviors we did not learn the skills to get along with children of our own age. Regardless of whether we were verbal or shy, we often chose to play with much younger children. With them we could either lead and be in charge or accept their much simpler rules of play. When we did play in the company of age-mates, our play was parallel to and not with them. We insisted on imposing our own rules, or we seemed to be 'in a world of our own'. Many of us had a hard time either winning or losing. Adults characterized our behavior as remote or distant. In some cases, we simply did not understand the rules. If we did understand them and realized they were needed for a game to work, if we had no interest in the game, we couldn't see any personal reward to joining in. At the time, the other children thought us arrogant and odd. And we were. When our parents or the playground teachers or our athletic coaches asked us to participate, we at first wanted 'in', but we often found ourselves saying and doing things that put us 'out'. Over time, we developed our own personal mantras to justify not participating.

Most of us were teased and bullied because we didn't fit in. Bullying and teasing by other children and adults did not prepare us well for adulthood. Adults tease too, although society does not usually call it that. Adult teasing takes on the various forms of derision, practical jokes, insults and other direct and indirect disrespect and discrimination. No adult wants to experience this. We have long memories of childhood teasing experiences, and they often affect our attitude towards 'adult play'. As AS adults, most of us tend to avoid social interaction and recreation with others. If we do develop healthy adult recreational habits – and many of us don't – we often adopt solitary activities that don't depend on involvement with others to be completely satisfying.

Many of us have a 'mind game' attitude towards recreation and leisure. Intellectually, we realize the benefit of exercise and healthy adult recreation. That's as far as many of us go with our thinking. It doesn't translate into a plan of action. We don't develop good habits because of our negative memories of old childhood experiences with recreation. Being dragged around thirty years later by childhood memories doesn't make much practical sense.

As adults, some of us learn the value and language of politeness. Others of us haven't learned, and we continue to express our refusal to participate in social activities with abrupt, negative language. Mentally, we recognize the value of a group experience but when others ask us to join, we resist. Our behavior has become automatic. In children, this behavior is labeled as 'defiant', 'resistant' and 'dysfunctional'. In adults, it is the behavior of refusal and of saying 'no' without really weighing the full consequence of our refusal. The result of our adult behavior being directed by childhood experience is our acting as though we have no choice in the matter.

We do.

The difference between adulthood and childhood lies in our power to make choices as adults that we did not have as children.

Perspective and change: What we see and what we don't see

In the early grades of school, educators recognize the importance of providing smooth transitions between activities for young students. As their world at school expands, neurotypical children learn to anticipate change and accept it. Their perspective broadens. Parents and special educators who work with AS students understand that it takes us longer to accept transitions, and adapt the learning environment and lesson materials to account for this. An AS child who is not adequately prepared for transitions remains unready to learn and stuck with a narrow perspective. That perspective means that our attention remains on ourselves. An accurate, though negative description that others use to refer to us under such circumstances is that we are self-centered. What many people don't see is that we are still trying to catch up. Persons always running to catch up remain breathless and are unable to appreciate what is going on around them.

A major cognitive and behavioral feature of Asperger Syndrome children and adults is our resistance to change. Experts in the field suggest that we crave a sense of control over our environment. We don't accept change until and unless we know the new situation is safe and we can exert control over it. If we remember our school experiences, many of us recall we had difficulty with transitions of all kind. As adults, we still do, although now we can call such transitions 'change'. One thing that distinguishes us from neurotypical control-lers is that we tend to objectify people and events. Experts also observe that we appear to be unfeeling in situations calling for empathy or awareness of the emotional states of others.

Most of us share a kind of intense and obsessive compulsivity for order and predictability, at least in parts of our life we can control. While other adults are given mental health label designations and referred to in such terms as 'anal retentive', there is something that distinguishes our desire for control from the orientation of others called 'control freaks'. Whereas control freaks wish to control others in a meglomaniacal way, our primary struggle is with controlling our environment and ourselves.

Many AS persons are not sensitive to others' boundaries because we are mentally unsure of our own. This cognitive phenomenon is demonstrated in AS children who reverse or confuse pronouns such as 'I/you' and 'he/she'. In adult life when some of us marry or form long-term bonds, most of us are considered by our partners to be distant or intrusive. More often we are a combination of both. Where we have families, we tend to close them to the outside world. If we have a neurotypical (NT) spouse, we often engage in pitched mental battles and physical struggles over how much social involvement and interaction we are 'expected' to have with our children and the outside world. Part of our need to 'keep it all in' is explainable by our desire to have control over our environment. It just so happens that our environment happens to include our mates and our children. For our partners and the other family members, such a pattern of non-involvement alternating with tight control is devastating. They never know 'where we are' from one minute to the next. We don't know either. Our failure to understand temporal, spatial and relationship boundary issues is often at the root of broken friendships, failed intimate and family member relationships, and divorce.

In social settings outside the family, other people characterize our failure to understand boundaries as our 'going too far' or not respecting others by being intrusive, excessively inquisitive or showing inappropriate familiarity with strangers or authority figures.

Several other common characteristics of AS affect our ability to be flexible and accept anything other than absolutes. We dislike unstructured situations. We think in black and white. Another social characteristic of persons with AS is a desire to follow rules coupled with a misunderstanding of the reason for the rules. Some of us become moral 'police' insisting that others follow all the rules.

As adults, some of us are attracted to employment that is substantially identified by our coworkers making and following rules for themselves and the public. Accounting, drafting and enforcement of procedures and policies, computer programming and system administration, archive and record-keeping activities, and certain warehousing and library functions are examples of fields of employment where rules are all-important.

Many of us are uncomfortable leaving our work incomplete or less than perfect. We also procrastinate. Many of us have a hard time making choices and decisions. This indecisiveness is a source of constant irritation to others. We often do not perceive their discomfort because we have not had formal training to be sensitive to it. Some of us do the opposite. We act impulsively, and then wonder why things don't work out. When others observe this, they attribute our behavior to things like a 'character flaw'. Impulsive behavior is retrainable in children. Although it is harder to accomplish, adults can be retrained as well.

Another cognitive feature of AS is our limited ability to generalize. As children we had difficulty in stepping outside of a situation to see the big picture. As educational assignments became increasingly complex, many of us had learning problems and study behaviors that showed we had difficulty forming concepts from a myriad of facts. This is commonly referred to by the metaphorical expression that 'we can't see the forest for the trees'.

Unless we were helped to think differently or disciplined ourselves to think otherwise then, many AS adults still have the same problem today. This phenomenon is often expressed in our social behavior. Many AS adults share a naiveté about people that often gets us in trouble. We have difficulty learning that a particular kind of person is responsible for a bad experience. When we next meet the same kind of person, we suffer the same disappointment without recognizing the pattern of events and warnings that made our first experience unpleasant.

The capacity to generalize depends on a related capacity to distinguish between experiences and events that are different. Our attention to detail often extends only to inanimate objects or things. Where this deficit can get us into trouble is when we can't perceive real differences between a present and a past *social* experience. Under these circumstances, it is as if our attention to detail and tendency to fixate on the past blocks out present information provided by all of our senses. We become, literally, blinded by the past.

AS children can be trained to be more aware of signs that a present event is not the same as a past one. So can we, but it is harder work. The work is harder because many of us have low expectations of ourselves after years of repeated bad judgment of other people. People who are concerned about us constantly tell us that 'we should know better'. Intellectually, we know that is true. Also true is the fact that many of us are literally clueless about how to learn to handle these matters differently. As adults we feel embarrassed telling others that we have this challenge. Even when we ask for help, many professional counselors have difficulty taking our requests for help seriously. Many counselors aren't experienced in training bright adults in 'the basics', yet it is that very training that will help us on our way. Unless we are frank with ourselves and recognize this need, we cannot advocate for ourselves when it comes time to make changes and improve our social skills.

Multi-tasking, learning and social skills

Motion

Ordinary childhood development involves activities progressing from rudimentary and simple to increasingly sophisticated and complex. As adults learn new things we follow the same path from simple to complex tasking. What characterized our development was its functional unevenness. Neuro-psychological evaluations of autistic children show this very clearly. When AS adults take full adult functional evaluations conducted by neuropsychologists familiar with AS, testing reveals that our development has remained uneven.

Researchers have found that the movements required for infants to roll over, sit and walk are differently executed by neurotypical children and children later diagnosed with autism. Smooth execution of those operations for infants as young as three months requires that multiple physical tasks be performed simultaneously and that they follow a consistent, uniform sequence. Re-searchers in one study likened these movements to a corkscrew motion with body parts following a sequenced, coordinated order as the infant turned over in its crib. Similar later observations about the fluidity and bilateralism of motion required for crawling and walking also revealed distinct differences between neurotypical infants and young children, and infants and children later diagnosed as autistic. The uncoordinated, clumsy movements displayed by infants later diagnosed with autism in performing these rudimentary physical tasks may be a very early diagnostic marker.

Eating

As infants, many of us were described as fussy eaters. The mere act of eating is an incredibly complex act. Only a short time following birth, eating is an exercise involving multiple senses and the coordination, in proper sequence, of many body muscle groups. As we mature, eating involves increasingly sophisticated communication of our need for food and reciprocal ways of involving others in satisfying that need. Every culture has developed elaborate eating rituals, and most of them involve multi-tasking. Those rituals involve very complex attitudes, expectations, behaviors and manners relating to preparing, serving, and the act of enjoying food. Even simple meals involve multi-tasking.

Eating is a social as well as a biological act. Some of us find the preparation of food for just ourselves to be a major task. Some of us find ourselves unable to eat without using certain rituals carried over from our childhood. With these behaviors in place, learning of 'manners' can be daunting and embarrassing. Since many of us spend a great deal of time alone, we often prefer to eat alone, even in places where eating alone is not a common practice. Eating alone can guarantee that we don't have to practice the complex social rituals of eating with others.

When we do dine out with others, we may have never learned or long ago forgotten the basic etiquette of handling eating implements and behavioral progression through the courses of a meal. As children, many of us were taught by our parents to follow their example when we were in doubt about the choice of a fork, or how to eat a particular food. Some of us 'got it'. Some of us didn't. As adults when we dine out with others, it is a difficult for us to find the right clues when searching for the rules of etiquette.

Multi-tasking, learning, and social skills

At each stage of our overall development we encounter demands to perform an increasing number of tasks simultaneously. The play of a very young child is simple, and often involves a single object or a few objects and functions.

We've already seen how play is a social act. During the first four years of childhood, NT children learn the majority of basic social skills they will need to become successful adults. The rules of play mirror the rules of non-play social interaction. If AS children are not formally trained in these rules, they do not learn them.

The play of older children is more complex. Academic learning follows the same route. Early learning uses mimicking and rote memory skills and concentrates on one or a few activities at a time. Advanced levels of school imposed demands that students understand and apply complex concepts and complete more difficult assignments. Those assignments require the student to work on a number of tasks simultaneously. This is called multi-tasking. As children get older, just as academic assignments get more complex, they are expected to engage in more complex social behavior. Solving increasingly complex social problems requires the same kind of multi-tasking.

AS children do not multi-task well. Neither do AS adults.

When many AS adults are asked to multi-task our thinking process – hence our working process – often slows way down. We become overwhelmed and overloaded. One of the first things to go when we are asked to multi-task is our ability to handle difficult social situations. Work often involves just such situations. When we are under stress, we revert to old behaviors. They get us into trouble. The higher functions of our brains shut down and we then operate in survival mode. If we are in the wrong place or the wrong job, operating at a survival mode level affects our work performance and efficiency. Sometimes we become so concerned about making additional mistakes or performing poorly that we become super cautious. If we look carefully we can see evidence of that same deliberation and caution operating in other areas of our life.

Remaining flexible

Many AS children and adults have non-verbal learning disabilities. However, we do learn. Best teaching practices acknowledge that creative students can arrive at a correct answer using different methods. We solve problems using eccentric means. In public education, class sizes have grown and teachers have many more administrative duties. These conditions often result in teachers not being able to vary their instruction techniques to meet our different learning styles. Because many of us did not learn basic social and communication skills essential for learning, many of us couldn't express our needs 'appropriately'. Many general education teachers no longer have the time or the training to teach social skills. The teaching of social skills has become a special education 'related service'.

AS children and adults have specific learning disabilities that impede our ability to understand when conditions of an assignment change or the rules governing a new assignment differ from old rules. When facing new situations, we remain 'stuck' and continue to use old methods and old rules that don't work. Unless we have good teachers or trainers who recognize our difficulty, many of us turn away from new learning opportunities. When we were children we acted out our frustration or found ways to stay away from a difficult class. Many of us were 'sick' a lot, an escape that allowed us to stay home when things overwhelmed us at school.

Many AS adults continue to apply out of date or inappropriate methods to resolve new problems or perform new tasks at work. Our 'stuckness' often takes the form of mental shutdown or our becoming increasingly rigid and inflexible in our responses to new challenges. Although many of us have learned good adaptive habits to deal with some of these challenges, others of us use adult variations of the dysfunctional behaviors we used when we were younger.

Some employers expect their workers to be creative and flexible problem solvers. Other employers still use authoritarian business practices calling for employees to follow lock-step methods of learning and performing new tasks that are alien to us. Our perseverant responses and behavioral reactions to change often get us into trouble.

Change

In closing this chapter, I return to the subject of change. Two prime attributes which employers look for in new employees and persons they retain and promote are flexibility in the face of change, and an ability to learn. The changing nature of corporate culture and the rapid change in the nature of work and the workforce itself has made these two attributes primary employee characteristics. Job security no longer exists even in areas traditionally considered safe, such as government and military work. Insecurity extends even to university level teaching. Employers can't offer security because events occur over which the person who hires and fires often has no control. Whole businesses get bought and sold. Whole departments vanish with lightening speed.

However unsettling this picture seems, other personal attributes such as reliability, dependability, consistency of work product, willingness to work hard under unfavorable, demanding circumstances, and even loyalty are still valued by employers. One more factor, one often difficult to quantify, may tip the balance in many personnel decisions involving hiring, promotion or retention. That factor is the employee's overall level of social skills. The skills involved are related to table manners or adherence to a dress code, but they are much more subtle. I refer to those skills deemed by employers to be essential to a smoothly operating work force however they define it.

If you are writing your employment biography, you will be asked to assess your social skills in Part 3 of this book.

Assessing your social skills

If you've come to this point in the chapter expecting answers from me about your own social skills, I am afraid I must disappoint you. Social skills, and your understanding of them, are completely contextual. Your skills 'operate' only in the presence of other persons, not by reading this book. The workbook questions in Part 3 are designed to help provide you with the answer you are looking for.

Most NT adults are not consciously aware of their observance of social rules and practice of many social skills because they have become 'automatic' much like routine driving behaviors or self-care habits. Most social rules are truly 'in the background'. Describing this background is somewhat like explaining the rules of grammar and syntax of a foreign language: you must 'get it right' in order to 'do it right'. Social rules, like language, do not operate in a vacuum. They are almost impossible to teach or learn 'in the abstract'. You can't learn them from a book because a book will never cover all the nuances of human experience in which social rules operate.

Like many of the procedures of work, many social rules tend to be invisible until they are broken. Learning about and using social rules appropriately is a subtle and life-long task. Depending on the context, speech consists of anywhere between 60 and 90 per cent non-verbal communication. Behavior and interactions between people are the major part of this communication, and social rules play a major role in good communication.

The physical placement of objects such as partitions and walls, the arrangement of objects in a physical setting such as chairs in a row instead of a circle or semi-circle reflect the web of social expectations and rules at work. The number of persons in a work setting also sets the social tone of a job. Working with just one other person may not call upon as many of these rules as working with more than one person. Whenever three or more people are involved in anything, politics and natural alliances automatically come into play. Extremely complex social interactions occur in these situations.

Jobs at the lower end of the social scale have more explicit, formally announced rules. Such rules are often printed in common areas, or mentioned frequently in employee meetings. The higher one climbs on the social ladder, the more unwritten and subtle the social rules become. There are many more formal and informal ones to observe. Learning and applying these rules correctly defines a person's social skill level.

If you have ever worked for someone else, the first thing that your employer encounters is your understanding of social skills. When supervisors conduct formal performance reviews, they often find it best to use soft phrases of commendation and criticism. Many of us miss the subtle meanings implicit in these words. Because of this, we could discount or overlook their real meaning. Since some of the meaning escapes us, we might not know which skills to improve or how to do it. We often leave a situation with an impression about what another person said without checking out our thoughts with them.

You can learn how to check your thoughts by practicing active listening skills. Some people come by active listening skills naturally, but most people, AS and neurotypical, benefit from formal instruction on how to listen well. You are not alone in wondering what other people think. By listening actively, you can monitor your thoughts as the conversation progresses. At the same time, active listening allows you a safe way to check out the thinking of the other person. Learning the meaning behind other people's words is a skill, and you are not going to learn it here. If you stay at the job for any length of time, it is unlikely that everyone's remarks to you are more negative than positive. This means you are doing something 'right'.

Much more likely is the scenario where people will give you mixed reports. If their remarks to you are long and involved, it may be difficult to distill the essence of their comments. As you listen to them, ask yourself, 'What are they really saying?' Your way of finding out what their real messages are will be unique to the situation and depend completely upon your relationship with the person(s) involved.

For us, learning social skills at an age far older than when they are ordinarily learned is a major challenge. Just because something is difficult doesn't mean that it is impossible. One of the advantages of being adult is that we can be creative about how we learn. We can seek out teachers and trainers who are sensitive to our eccentricities and can help us use them in learning social skills. Once we master some of the social skills we lack, no one else has to know what we went through to get there.

For the purpose of completing your employment biography, all you need to do is recall the other person's words. Instructions in Part 2 will provide you with guidance in how to do that.

CHAPTER 4

Learning and Work Styles

Our learning challenges and their relationship to co morbid conditions

Assistive technology

A word of explanation before we proceed. 'Co morbid' is the medical term that in plain English refers to the co-existence of a second or many other medically diagnosed conditions in the same person. AS itself is a multiple-manifestation condition. That is what having a 'syndrome' means. It is perfectly possible for a secondary condition to become dominant under conditions of stress or for other reasons. That fact does not mean we are any less AS at the same time. Thus, when we say we have AS, it often means that we have other conditions which affect certain functions, but are not as prominent as the overall, pervasive, lifelong character of Asperger Syndrome.

DYSGRAPHIA

Due to recent developments in learning theory and demonstrations of effective, alternative instructional methods, public educators have begun to understand just how out of date is their understanding of how children actually learn. As an example of how out of date thinking can radically affect the education of a child with a developmental disability, let's take the example of a fine motor deficit and its obvious 'educational' manifestation – difficulty with writing (dysgraphia). Assistive technology evaluators and occupational therapists may recommend the use of a keyboard or a laptop computer with voice recognition software for a student with dysgraphia to compose his school assignments. Right off, some teachers resist the abstract notion of the student's need for this assistive technology. When the technology is provided to the student, they resist learning how to use it so the student can be instructed in its use. Let's assume some progress is made in that department. They then restrict its use only to their classroom or say it can't be used in their classroom at all. The student must use it in the 'resource room'. They forbid the student to take the technology into other classes or take it home to do his other assignments. There is one fundamental problem with this kind of thinking. The school may have bought the assistive technology, but the student 'owns it'. It is essential for his learning. Refusal to see this demonstrates that the teacher or the school has a 'control issue', not an educational one.

If this same behavior took place with an adult and a needed piece of technology such as a wheelchair or Braille typewriter, could you imagine the response? What's the difference? I'll tell you. The student has a hidden learning disability. The adult has a noticeable sensory or mobility disability.

It has been repeatedly demonstrated that appropriate assistive technology of all kinds, high tech and low tech, makes it possible for disabled students to achieve the same degree of subject mastery as their non-disabled peers. Administrator and teacher resistance to assistive technology has nothing to do with this fact. Their resistance is all about power and control.

Many AS individuals find the act of writing a major challenge. We often spend so much time concentrating on how to write that the content and meaning of our work suffers. We find ourselves wanting to make our letters perfect and to correct every tiny mistake. If you haul your school homework out of the attic storage where your parents may have kept it, you might notice that your written pages are worn through with eraser holes or cross-outs. My schoolwork looked like that. Teachers mistake this problem for other things. Many grade school teachers insist on the importance of good handwriting. Some students with AS may have less difficulty with printing, but when it comes to learning cursive handwriting, we go all to pieces. While our difficulty with cursive writing is called dysgraphia, other conditions may contribute to it. Stress is a major one.

If our challenge is recognized for what it really is, it can be worked with. Some AS children benefit from sensory integration training, others benefit from the techniques of occupational therapy and physical therapy, and others experience advances in function from vision training. If none of these approaches remediate our fine motor deficit, our challenges may be side-stepped with keyboards, laptop computers and voice recognition software. While spelling and grammar are essential to good communication, children who have substantial reading and writing challenges find the spell-check and grammar correcting features of any good word processing program essential to completing their assignments. Learning how to use these basic tools in a word processing program is as essential as learning how to type.

Students who can't type for reasons related to their disabilities now have voice recognition software that allows them to complete their assignments in written form by using the computer as an electronic transcription device. Rather than continue to insist that children who can't write or spell well master both skills through horrific manual exercises and endless hours of rote memorization, some educators have seen the light and are abandoning demands that we perform skills made less essential in the age of computers.

DYSCALCULIA

I know of some employers who require their applicants to complete mathematical operations by hand without the use of a calculator as a part of the job application. Other employers require the applicant to show mastery of ten key calculators. Yet others want the applicant to demonstrate mastery of advanced mathematical reasoning. Many college aptitude and placement tests do the same.

Dyscalculia, or a functional incapacity to perform mathematical calculations, is also a recognized specific learning disability. A lot of AS folks can't 'calculate' their way out of a wet paper sack. I found my mathematical brick wall way back in the third grade when trying to understand long division. To this day, I am a mathematical basket case. Calculators are cheap and effective assistive technology devices designed to assist non-impaired individuals perform these tasks. More and more educators recognize the lunacy of forcing children to rote-learn and memorize data and functions that in the real world of post secondary education and business are performed automatically and electronically on business machines and computer programs. Some AS persons perform rote mathematical operations with ease yet balk at more complex operations, while others can perform advanced complex mathematics with ease but cannot master basic math. As long as educators insist on a lock-step method of learning, many of us find our real abilities thwarted.

One of the first questions asked by employers now is whether the applicant has computer skills. The question implies that the applicant knows how to type and is familiar with basic computer applications, basic math available one way or the other, word processing and data processing experience.

AUDITORY AND VISION PROCESSING DISORDERS

Some AS students have other conditions which hinder their ability to learn. When AS children delay their answers in response to questions, or hear only part of the question, or don't hear it at all, they may a condition known as central auditory processing disorder (CAPD). This is a neurobiological condition. The brain garbles and delays the process between hearing something, understanding it (processing) and then making the appropriate response. The hearing tests performed by regular school audiologists are not designed to detect CAPD. Audiologists professionally trained to diagnose the condition and evaluate how severely it affects the person's ability to function in the world of spoken communication can identify this condition. There is electronic technology designed to reduce background noise and focus the person's attention on a single speaker. It has been around in increasingly miniaturized versions for fifteen years. There are promising therapeutic approaches which help with some of the sensory issues related to this condition. The most notable one is Auditory Integration Training (AIT) and its variants following the general model developed by Dr Guy Berard.

OTHER SENSORY ISSUES

Many AS children and adults have problems with sensory sensitivity. Some of us are especially sensitive to noise. Light, textures, tastes, smells, and other sensory input can cause our nervous systems to shut down. When we are in a condition of overwhelming sensory input, we find our ability to function is affected at different levels of severity. Successful integration of sensory information in the brain is an essential condition for learning. Sensory Integration Training, following the work of Dr. Jean Ayres has proven an effective technique in desensitizing some children's responses to certain stimuli that interfere with communication and learning. It also allows them to use all of their senses to learn, and to favor those senses that appear to be most efficiently used by the brain to learn. Research confirms that this sensory mix recipe is different for every person.

I know a little something about auditory hypersensitivity. I have a touch of it. I have been interested in high fidelity sound since I built my first amplifier (with help) at the age of 13. I have no money now, but at one time I had sound equipment that would make the average consumer fall over in a dead faint. My hearing was so acute, and still is, that I can tell you the make of piano being played on a recording. I know microphones to the point that I can tell you what kind of mike is used and where it is placed when I listen to recordings. I have an auditory memory that doesn't stop. However, when I am in a noisy environment, I find it almost impossible to concentrate on what someone is saying. I get so upset by the noise of other people or particular sounds that my mind literally shuts down. I get extremely agitated. Unless the auditory distraction is removed or I move away, I cannot continue the conversation or my train of thought.

Some children with AS also have central vision processing disorder (CVPD). This is a condition similar to CAPD in that the brain does not properly process the sensory information sent from the eyes. This disorder has nothing to do with how 'well' the child sees according to the Snellen chart. Vision testing in schools is usually limited to that instrument alone. CVPD is detectable by the testing and evaluation of behavioral optometrists, professionals specifically trained to diagnose, evaluate, and treat this disorder. If one has it, this may have profound effects on the person's ability to read or process complex thoughts presented by the act of reading. Filtered eyeglass lenses, Irlen lenses, may have some effect on children and adults who are sensitive to certain spectrum backgrounds. For some people CVPD is treatable through vision therapy, a sequence of exercises easily learned by the youngest of children and the oldest of adults. The effect of training is often nothing short of miraculous. In combination with specific phonemic decoding reading methodologies such as Orton-Gillingham and Lindamood Bell and their variants, vision therapy can produce substantial gains in comprehension and reading speed. As with any other therapies and methodologies, the success of each approach varies from individual to individual. There is enough information on both remediation techniques to warrant acceptance by doubting school officials.

DYSLEXIA

Dyslexia is a general term used to describe a myriad of conditions responsible for reading difficulties. Dyslexia appears more frequently in the AS population than in the neurotypical population. Dyslexia impedes or scrambles complex information processing, and some researchers feel that for many kinds of learning to take place, the brain depends both upon sight and sound to be successfully integrated. A variety of techniques are used to remediate this condition. It is true that some children don't benefit by them. But a particular child is not *some* children. He or she is *this* child. Some administrators call determining whether one technique works when another doesn't 'experimentation'. To conscientious teachers and many parents, it is called a 'good teaching practice'.

Other co morbid conditions can accompany Asperger Syndrome. It isn't possible to review them all here.

Other barriers to learning: Seizure disorders, 'stims' and depression

Until recently, medical authorities thought that seizures in non-epileptic children occurred once the child attained a certain, advanced age. Now, brain scan technology identifies seizure disorders at increasingly younger ages. Mild seizure brain activity can be spotted in very young autistic children. Some of the 'spacing out' activity of persons with AS is actually mild seizure behavior. At the onset of puberty, some AS children develop pronounced seizure activity behavior. The seizures need not be of grand mal severity to have an impact in settings where adolescents are very conscious of differences at an age of peer conformity. For the most part, seizures can be partially controlled or reduced in frequency with medication. Some milder seizure activity can disappear as our brains approach the physical limits of their growth in late adolescence. The exact reason for this disappearance of once unsettling behavior is unknown.

Self-stimulatory behavior, or 'stims', are another common diagnostic feature of Asperger Syndrome. In their mildest expression, stims can take the form of spinning or twirling, or fascination with twirling inanimate objects. In school, a child's stims can be quite distracting. Some children have positively revolting stim behaviors. However, they usually can be 'reshaped'. There is some confusion over nail-biting. It does seem to be common with some of us. Until recently I've worked in jobs where that aspect of my personal appearance wasn't too important. That's not the case now. Just when I think I have it under control, I find myself munching away. It definitely has a comforting effect, but carried to the extreme it can be considered 'self-injurious behavior'. That's a separate category, but a few of us still do that as well.

Elaborate behavioral rituals sometimes accompany stim behavior. Unenlightened diagnosticians label us obsessive-compulsive because of the ritual character of this behavior. We also form attachments to certain objects and find them essential to our sense of well-being. In school we often couldn't learn without them being present or close by. They took up a lot of our time, but ironically were essential for our feeling comfortable enough to learn. At work, some of us have to be surrounded by our familiar objects, or have our workspaces arranged 'just so' before we can work. While this looks like obsessive-compulsive behavior, it really isn't. It is a reflection of our need to have comforting 'patterns'. Many of us find it necessary to start work from this kind of a pattern template.

When we are under average amounts of stress, stims rarely return; but under conditions of profound distress, very early stims can reappear. At the end of my cabinetmaking career I became so distressed on a few occasions that I found myself beating the side of my head with my open hands. I was so 'out of it' that I didn't care who saw me. That was something I hadn't done since I was in tenth or eleventh grade.

Many adults continue stimming behavior, but have found ways to do it without being observed. Sometimes we copy common behaviors of others, such as pencil tapping and twiddling with objects in our hands when we are bored. We often 'shed' our stims. This isn't because our neurobiolgical need for such behavior ceases. A good number of adults with AS report their need for this activity, and their frustration and increased irritability when in environments which don't allow for stim expression. This continued need may account for our preference for types of living and work arrangements that guaranty of privacy so we are free to 'be ourselves'.

Until very recently, medical science insisted that depression was a disorder whose onset took place relatively late at life. With new discoveries about the brain and just using common sense, pediatricians and parents can identify depression in very young children. One condition always present in persons diagnosed with Asperger Syndrome is a low, constant level of depression called dysthymia. Unrecognized and untreated, severe depression can lead to childhood, adolescent and adult suicide. Twenty-five years before I knew I was autistic, I underwent a kind of therapy that prompted me to go back to our family albums and study childhood photographs. There it was. It was unmistakable. From family photographs, I recognized my depressed state even in early infancy. Photographs of my face as an infant showed a flat or clearly depressed state in settings where the faces of others were animated and expressive. People with AS are identified through family histories and reports of depressed behavior. Many of us went through childhood and adolescence with undiagnosed depression. Medical science recognizes that depression has a neurobiological basis. When depression remains unrecognized and untreated in adults, it can severely affect our ability to learn; account for poor work performance, lost days of work, lost jobs, loss of friends; and cause alcohol and drug abuse. In many cases depression can be successfully treated with medication and talk therapy. Talk therapy does not work for most of us, so medication combined with other good health habits may be one answer. Adults for whom depression has been an issue often find we must accept the fact that we may be on anti-depressants for the rest of our lives. Some of us have found this medication as essential to our well being as insulin is for persons with diabetes.

Understanding how you learn

Most of us do not spend much time thinking about how we learn. It is as important to understand how we do *not* learn as it is to know how we best learn.

Because people learn in different ways, there is no 'one best way' to learn. Methods for instruction and training others often fail to work effectively for us. Learning involves the use of all senses. For persons having a weak or undeveloped critical sense such as hearing or sight, learning is sometimes difficult. Many children with AS have difficulty integrating all of their senses into the learning experience.

One feature of AS commonly reported for children and adults is unusual sensitivity, either hypersensitivity (excessive) or hyposensitivity (very low). For many AS persons, sensory overload or insensitivity to certain stimuli makes functioning in some environments very difficult. In the case of hypersensitivity, the persons with AS may perceive the stimuli as an assault and react accordingly. As long as the stimulus remains and the person is not desensitized to it or fails to find a way to deal with it, learning may be difficult or impossible. In the case of adults with low sensitivity, we may unknowingly work in an unsafe environment, or develop a work practice that can be dangerous to others or ourselves.

The rate at which we learn also varies. Our learning rate is dependent on a number of factors. Some of these factors belong under the heading of 'executive function'. Some examples are the way in which we solve problems, organize our time, organize our work, plan and sequence activities to accomplish a task, react to and manipulate our environment, determine our priorities, communicate with others, and relate to others in while in a learning setting.

Whenever parents and educators notice learning difficulties related to our rate of performance, they often devise alternate methods and environments for training and instruction. Students with AS also develop their own effective alternative methods for learning. They may be very unorthodox, but they work. Observant parents and educators then help the student generalize these techniques to other subject matter and other challenges.

What you learn and how you learn it

Before you begin your own description of how you learned specific tasks, it might be helpful to understand a little more about the concept of multiple intelligence. In 1983, Howard Gardner formalized a theory about how people learn. Knowing that individuals learn differently, he proposed seven categories or styles of learning. An eighth has been recently added. Here they are in a list, with a brief description of each.

- *Logical/mathematical intelligence.* This involves reasoning and logical thinking, discovery of patterns and relationships, curiosity about natural events, and a 'scientific' outlook emphasizing controlled experimentation.

- *Interpersonal intelligence.* This is social intelligence. Empathy with others, natural leadership, people-organizing and manipulation, common sense, and great sensitivity to others and their feelings are prominent as personal strengths.

- *Bodily kinesthetic intelligence.* Some manifestations are hyperactivity, gross and fine motor agility, high dependence on sensory information for learning, skill in using hunches and 'gut feelings' and expression through acting and theatre skills.

- *Musical/rhythmic intelligence.* This kind of intelligence involves thinking in sounds, rhymes and aural patterns; and immediate response to music and expressive with music, high sensitivity to environmental sounds, and responding to aural differences and noises others find imperceptible.

- *Intrapersonal.* This intelligence refers to unusually good self-knowledge and ability to focus inwardly, high awareness of inner feelings, dreams, ideas, analytical, and often involves avoidance of team activities. Persons with this intelligence have a strong need for privacy and are zealous about their need for personal time.

- *Linguistic/verbal intelligence.* People with this kind of intelligence think in words, are highly verbal and write well, are good at story-telling, have critical auditory skills, enjoy wordplay and languages, and are jokesters and avid readers.

- *Spatial/visual intelligence.* Persons with this kind of intelligence think visually or in images, are able to visualize and represent things clearly, know exact locations, have great mechanical curiosity and skill in designing hardware and contraptions.

- *Naturalist intelligence.* This intelligence involves a strong sense of unity with the natural world of plants and animals, sensitivity to animal intelligence and moods, preference for natural aesthetics, and interest in restoration, environmental repair and wholeness.

The concept of multiple intelligences implies that not only do people learn differently, but also that their combination of learning styles requires educators and trainers to be sensitive to each person's peak learning performance profile.

In Part 3 you will answer a number of questions that will help you to understand your learning style. The objective of the exercise is demonstrate how complex learning can be, and that if you've 'made it so far', you've done so by learning. One thing is for sure. You won't come up with wrong answers, but in the process of discovery of 'what went wrong', in some learning situations, you might learn how to avoid the tasks where learning proved difficult or to adopt a new approach to learning once you recognize that that approach may have worked for you at one time. We often forget our successes because we ruminate so much on our failures. I am a firm believer that all experience, regardless of how bad it is, offers positive lessons.

One observation I carry with me comes from a study of mid level business executives who were asked to rate their competence. Those judged by their superiors to be ineffective managers always gave themselves far higher competence scores than supervisors who were also asked to rate these managers. When asked questions about how they learned, few of the incompetent managers mentioned their mistakes as good lessons. Managers considered the most successful by their fellow managers and their supervisors were those who consistently felt themselves to be only moderately competent. The one thing that made them stand out to their supervisors, and about which they felt most positive, was that they learned more from their mistakes than from their accomplishments.

Because of our makeup, most of us probably would make bad managers, but not for the reasons I've outlined above. Most of us don't see ourselves as 'management types'. The one person we can manage, even if we don't manage others, is ourselves. In order to do that, we can learn as much as we can about how we learn. Once we understand more about that, we can seek knowledge more efficiently.

Going for help

The information in the following pages is more valuable to you if you have completed your employment biography. If you leap ahead to look for trainers and teachers without having determined the precise nature of your learning needs your outcome from any training experiences may remain unfocused and lack a clear 'next step'.

Many of the suggestions I make are tied to earlier observations about special education and the effect that industry has had upon adult service agencies. The type of education and training you will be seeking is different than what you have experienced in the past. You will be in charge of the design of your program, just as you have been in charge of writing your own employment history. You get to drive the bus. This is your journey, and you even get to punch the tickets. The answers you give to questions asked in the workbook can be markers on the roadmap you draw. You can set the pace of learning, and from what you know about yourself, you may already have determined your priorities and ultimate goals. The training or education you seek should be designed to help you achieve benchmark objectives along the way. In the language of special education: 'You are in charge of your own IEP'.

After completing your employment biography, you might consider consulting a traditional professional to help you with learning or performance issues. Just because a person has a 'PhD' (doctor's degree) at the end of their professional name does not mean they are effective or understand the significance of practical problem-solving work with their clients or patients. The work you may be willing to do is highly practical and it involves real problems you experienced and are still dealing with.

If you have learning challenges, many community colleges and four-year schools offer courses on how develop effective study habits. While some of these courses are focused on academics, many of the techniques are equally applicable to learning real-life work tasks. Because many of us have learning disabilities, we may need more individualized training to improve our study habits. It is available. Ask for it. Disabled students services offices in both kinds of institutions often have learning disability specialists available to work one-on-one with you. In community colleges especially, other coursework is available at low cost for personal development in such areas as overcoming shyness, assertiveness training, and basic business etiquette.

Ordinarily, one would not think of going to a college campus to learn how to resolve workplace learning and performance problems. Adults out of school are supposed to know how to tackle them. People with AS are 'supposed' to know a lot of things we don't. Organizational skills we fail to exercise at work are similar to the organizational skills we may have had trouble with in school. Some of us taking adult education classes discover that the passage of time hasn't helped us get beyond our old study habit barriers.

Adult learning disability counseling can help us past them by training us to break down complex tasks into manageable, accomplishable ones. The field of continuing adult education has developed parallel with the field of special education for children in K-12. Unlike schoolchildren who are captives of a single system, we can choose among a variety of educational, training, and personal development courses. If one approach doesn't work, as adults, we can choose others. The author of this book is a firm believer in 'anything that works'.

One reliable source for adult self-improvement and personal development training is the community or junior college system. Public libraries and other educational institutions have catalogues and course schedules. If you receive these materials in the mail, rather than discarding them unread, check out the courses shown in the 'adult learning', extension', and 'personal development' listings. As a rule, these courses are well taught and highly practical. Community colleges work on a consumer-satisfaction model. Bad teachers and bad courses don't survive long under the scrutiny of student and sponsor evaluation forms.

There are other sources for adult learning and training for adults that treat you with dignity and respect. A whole industry of private trainers has developed over the past 30 years. A majority of such persons work in the business world in the field of training and organizational development. Many of these same trainers are available as personal trainers and coaches to members of the public, just as they act as private consultants to business executives. Many trainers are former teachers, social workers, and ministers. Most professional trainers and educators of this kind try to develop niche market specialties. They often look for persons to help them rehearse their approach and skills.

You might meet some of them as presenters in free community education courses offered by public libraries, community colleges, and the adult education divisions of large school districts. While they are paid for their public presentations, the presentations often provide them with opportunities to experiment on a broad, non-paying public before they start charging substantial fees for their services in the private market. If you attend such free lectures you might wish to speak with a presenter and ask if she would be willing to take you on as a client. Since she may still be at the learning stage of working with new training techniques, she could take you on as a 'learn with me' client. There is no guarantee that such work would be successful for you, but it never hurts to ask. The worst that can happen is a 'No' answer.

There is another advantage to consider in personal training work with these professionals. Many of them are highly practical. They are paid to produce results in a competitive market. If they don't do a good job, their 'customers' shop around for others who can deliver effective service. Many of them are open to new knowledge, unlike many of their traditional colleagues. Even if they are professionally trained, they often practice in very untraditional settings. In a word, they are hustlers, in the good sense of the term. Hustling doesn't make them rogues. They are often at the cutting edge of what is possible for professionals with their training and experience.

A warning is in order.

Some of the most effective trainers and private educators don't have PhDs behind their names. Many of them don't have expensive offices or high hourly fee structures. They work in a rapidly developing field. Even if they receive their training in a traditional manner, if you are thinking of seeking their help you should check them out before committing yourself to work with them. Ask for references to other professionals who know about them and their work. If you can, ask to speak to former clients or students. If they have taught in a formal institutional setting, check with the department head where they taught or still teach. If they are teaching in such places now, talk with some of their current students and get a sense of how effective they are as educators and trainers. As in choosing any professional for personal work, be a cautious and prudent consumer.

CHAPTER 5

Interests, Skills and Talents

Interests are things about which you are curious and want to learn more. Persons with AS are described by others as having limited interests. That might be true for any given time, but over our life times we may have developed many areas of knowledge and expertise that we no longer use. Recalling them, even if they are not current, helps us recognize just how rich our knowledge and skill base really is.

Skills are developed through training, education and experience. A person can start from a zero knowledge and competency base and become skilled. Whether it is in school or at work, when you feel as though you have 'settled in', your feelings reflect your sense of competency in handling the tasks. You have learned some or most of the necessary skills to perform those tasks. Skills are transferable to other tasks and other jobs.

Talent is innate, not acquired. People usually have more than one talent. With our talents we do not start from a zero base of competence or knowledge. A good example of how talent works is found with gifted musicians. While many persons can play an instrument, people know when they are in the presence of true talent. Anyone who coaches persons in a specialization can spot it. Faced with a person with talent, a good coach or teacher works *with* something that is already present, honing and refining the student's natural abilities. The best teachers allow the person's own style to flourish. The different styles of persons with talent are what set them apart from their talented equals.

If you will be writing your employment biography by completing the workbook in Part 3, your first task in the workbook section dealing with this topic will be to write down a list of all your interests, skills and talents. When considering employment, each of these things can be considered a personal asset.

Many people with AS discount these assets. Because we can't perfect them in the way we want, we dismiss many of them and lose track of others. If other people think we don't have the skill level to perform a particular job, some of us may assume that our skill is useless altogether. We might have had these feelings very early in our schooling, or have them from something someone said just yesterday about our performance. If we take the criticism seriously, personally, and as an absolute statement, we may not be motivated to improve the skill. Sometimes life's events suddenly call upon us to summon up long discarded or unused skills. We may be in a situation where no one has even the small amount of skill we developed. Suddenly, people need our skill to get things accomplished that are important to them. We start feeling that we can do it, and that motivation is enough for us to pick up from where we left off. Then we feel competent and capable of learning. People of great value to us don't criticize us if our performance isn't perfect. The reason: it's better than what they can do. We feel needed and validated.

Other people can't see the value of some of our interests. Faced with such negativity, we may abandon the interest. Sometimes, however, we just grow out of it. Some of us don't care what others think and we've kept those interests in one form or another all of our lives. Others of us maintain our interest, but express it in activities that are 'age appropriate'. A good example is an interest in maps and directions. As children, we were talking road maps. We knew where things were because we studied where they were all the time. Having that same level of intensity during our middle school and high school years made other students call us nerds. It was true. We were. Then in college or if we were interested in hiking or nature, we get a brilliant idea: How about learning to be a cartographer, a person who draws and studies maps for a living? There you have it. An interest turned into one person's life work. Another example of an intense specialized interest turned into work is college teaching or becoming an academic professional. There we can engage in pursuit of our arcane bits of knowledge all we want, write and lecture about it, be real 'grown up professors' and get paid for it. The best part of it is that people don't make fun of us any more. And if they do, we can laugh about it because we are in the company of many others like ourselves.

When we were children we often expressed our talents precociously and naturally. We had fun. Then came the serious bit. Our parents knew that talents could be further developed through learning or training. They pushed us. What about lessons? That's when some of us got into trouble. Maybe we had bad teachers. Maybe we expected too much of ourselves. We're known to do that. Then either our teacher or our 'perfectionist' told us that just as we were, we weren't as good as someone else. Our black and white thinking told us that since that was the case, we weren't talented at all. The fun stopped. We didn't know that there were other teachers out there who could inspire us. Many of us stopped right there.

Our talents operate in the same way. Again, because we are such perfectionists, we discount what talents we have. Here is black and white thinking again: 'If I can't be the best, then I'm nobody'. One thing is interesting about our black and white thinking. We may have thought one way when we were younger. We can learn to think in gradations. As we mature, we see other people with varying degrees of talent sometimes making perfect fools of themselves but enjoying it. As adults, most of us have learned that it isn't polite to criticize others because they aren't doing something perfectly. What's wrong with softening our criticism of ourselves? Some of us do. We pick up old talents and we run with them. Some of us start piano lessons at the age of fifty. Others of us remember the joy of something else we abandoned because we couldn't do it perfectly when we were children and pick it up again. Painting and art are examples. So is writing.

Teachers who instruct adult students know that they can't work with them the same way they do untalented children. Many of these teachers are professionals. They teach what they love. They teach because they have a faith that others share their same passion. They know that their adult students crave the enjoyment they may once have had, and lost. They rekindle the passion with patience, perseverance, and encouragement.

Here's an example of talent put aside, ready to become a part of my life once more.

I am a passionate listener of classical music. When I was a child, although I never learned to sight-read I could hear the harmonies and progressions in complicated music and play them on the family piano. I used to spend hours at the piano often working through depression and channeling its energy into musical expression. I can remember the instrumental parts in complex orchestral scores. Although I can't read a score, I know exactly when different conductors directing the same piece of music change single instrument or section voicing. I stopped playing the piano when I became a young adult because I was embarrassed that I wasn't as good as the original source of my inspirations. To this day I have an ear for good performance and am a knowledgeable person in the field of classical music. Although I've owned several homes, I've always repressed my desire to buy or rent a piano and continue playing, this time with lessons from a patient teacher. I so brainwashed myself into thinking I could not be a world-class pianist that I gave up the immense personal pleasure my childhood playing brought me.

A number of years ago when I just moved to Portland, Oregon from San Francisco, I missed being able to play so badly that I toyed with the idea of learning to play the cello, my favorite string instrument. One day I summoned the courage to go down to a violinmaker's shop and try out a cello. I had already contacted two teachers, each of whom was interested in taking me on as a student. I told them that when I was in high school, I had sat in an empty schoolroom with a school orchestra cello and noodled along with Pablo Casals performing the Bach suites for unaccompanied cello. I arrived breathless at the store, climbed the seven floors to the violinmaker's shop, selected an instrument, and the owner showed me to a large, glassed-in studio. He had tuned the instrument. I sat in the chair with this instrument between my knees and the bow in my hand. I could not touch bow to strings. I was petrified with fear and anxiety about what would come out. It wouldn't be Schiff or Maisky or Rostropovitch or Yo-Yo Ma. It would be the scratchy sound of a fool with a carved box between his legs and a stick with horsehair in his hand. After five minutes of exquisite agony I started to weep. It wouldn't happen then, I said to myself. I 'collected my emotions', returned to the counter and thanked the owner. I mumbled something about not being ready. He understood. I really didn't.

I do now. I have a sense that things are about to change.

CHAPTER 6

My Work and Asperger Syndrome

In Appendix I, I've drawn up a list of Asperger Syndrome characteristics. If you choose to write your employment biography using the workbook in Part 3, the list is designed as a checklist to help you identify which of those behaviors, manifestations, or features of your AS are connected with your work life.

From this point forward, I use the terms 'characteristics', 'behavior', and 'manifestation' to mean the same thing. As I state in the introductory paragraph to the list, it is not to be used for diagnostic purposes. The entries on the list correspond with manifestations frequently mentioned by individuals with AS. They also come from anecdotal descriptions offered by medical, counseling, occupational therapy, speech and language pathology, and education professionals who understand AS. If you are a casual reader to this book, consider the list of Asperger Syndrome characteristics only as a list. Don't form impressions of people only based on parts *you* want to see. An autistic person is far more than a mere sum of the 'parts' on that list.

Only where such behaviors are mentioned by at least two or more experts in the AS field or by numerous AS adults do I list it as an AS characteristic. Remember that individuals with Asperger Syndrome need not share all of these characteristics to be diagnosed as AS. Some characteristics may not have been prominent and may not have been a problem for you in your job. But you know that certain conditions in your life produce stress, causing behaviors bothersome to you or others.

The meaning of words

Before you begin, a note of caution. The list contains manifestations that most neurotypical people consider as negative. As verbal people, we take many of our cues about the world from words and their meaning. For several years at the close of the last decade there was a heated debate among people with AS to come up with a new vocabulary to describe who we are and how others in the greater society should refer to us. These debates occur periodically and are a function of a reawakening of people's consciousness about the connection between labels and the social positions of those who are labeled.

The debate generally hinges around the power of words, and who has control over coining the words to describe others. With mental illnesses, the terms used to describe the illness have been the exclusive purview of medical professionals. Professionals in education, rehabilitation and counseling adopt those words as convenient handles. When the words are neutral and non-derogatory in their application there isn't any problem with their use. We all know what happens when labels are misused. People in the movement for civil rights of people with mental illness have made this an issue for six decades. Society resists correcting the negative connotations attached to words describing mental illness. Calling a mental illness something else, or calling a person who has a mental illness a 'person with' the illness, or any other efforts to go 'politically correct' with nomenclature usually fall flat and ring hollow. The real issue is not in changing the words. The real issue lies in changing attitudes.

Asperger Syndrome is not a mental illness. It is a neurobiological condition characterized by differences in cognitive processing with attendant behavioral outcomes. The old sage, 'Sticks and stones may break my bones, but words will never hurt me' doesn't work for those who words actually do hurt. Since many of us have been so badly labeled and misdiagnosed in the past, words the experts coin to describe us take on a special charge.

The forces in our society who control a the language won't easily relinquish their license to label. If the labels are loaded with meanings synonymous with social disapproval, moral turpitude, or terms such as 'defiance', 'resistance', 'stubbornness', 'insensitivity', and the like, we have a right to be angry when we know these meanings are attached to descriptions of us by people who don't understand autistic behavior. In many cases, these terms are used to describe our response to persons in positions of authority. Some psychiatric terms are power words used by persons of authority to strip patients and clients of their dignity and respect as individuals.

In the end, it may be up to us to wrest control of the words used in describing ourselves – how we are to be viewed by ourselves and others – away from those whose professions and practices have coined the power words of medicine, special needs education and rehabilitation. For the time being, engaging in such work as we try to sort out the significance of our flavors of AS in our life as workers may not be helpful. If we go on such a quest in the middle of exploring our work history, we will become distracted from the main task of determining what works in our lives. Don't go into consulting situations with professionals eager to pick a fight. You may win the skirmish but lose the war. The only time these matters should become important is when you encounter negativity, disinterest, or a total lack of understanding. Challenge is appropriate if the weight of their words starts to drag you down.

Thinking in categories

It is not uncommon to hear doctors and other experts refer to us as people who 'suffer from Asperger Syndrome'. Personally, I find that phrase repugnant. At a certain stage in thinking about my AS, I decided that what I 'suffer' from is that professional attitude. My personal and work life is affected by particular manifestations of my AS. Specific learning disabilities and disorganization are big issues for me. Temper is another one.

In most daily activities, neurotypical people muddle along. Somehow, despite the labels, adults with AS manage to muddle along too. And some people get along rather well, thank you. I do. And I'm sure you do as well.

Remember that the medical profession, and to a great extent psychologists and other specialists dealing with exceptional people, take on a certain mind-frame to do their work. As we have seen in reviewing the attitudes of policy makers in the public schools, most school administrators still think of persons with disabilities as second-class students. They see us as labels, as categories, as classes of persons. School administrators are authority figures, and so their attitudes are reflective of other opinion leaders in the adult world.

It isn't uncommon for other professionals to put us into categories. It makes their work easier. It is essential for professionals to have a healthy sense of distance from their clients, otherwise they'd have no lives of their own. That same distance can also blind them to some of the uniqueness of each client or patient they see. When we encounter professionals who think too categorically when working with us over work issues, their attitude can influence the way we think of ourselves. Many of us adopt the worst side of their categorical thinking and end up in second-class work.

Bear in mind that we are not our manifestations. They are not what define us as persons. I'd like to use the words of a powerful advocate for autistic persons. Jim Sinclair dislikes the term 'a person with'. I agree with him. Here is the argument: One would hardly think of a blind person as a 'person with blindness', or a person with multiple sclerosis as a 'person with multiple scleroisness.' I am an autistic person. Autism does not define me, but it goes a long way to 'explain' me to myself and to others. It explains the similarity of my conduct with that of others in the same boat. We all handle our oars differently, even if we pull in the same direction. Autism does not explain the uniqueness of my being. My experience does that. Your experience explains your uniqueness. As a final way of looking at this issue, think of an apartment block. Imagine a situation where the manager, for her convenience, puts all the short people together as roommates. Then all the blind people. Then all the people with brown eyes. Then everyone who is left-handed. A pretty strange living arrangement, would you not agree? We are as different from one another as we are from neurotypical persons who are also different from one another. Broad brushes work when one paints a barn wall. We aren't barns.

One last thing. Many characteristics of AS, when carried to extremes, are dysfunctional for you and for everyone else. Others can be beneficial in certain settings. If you are a contemplative person, rumination, attention to detail, intellectualizing, and other cognitive characteristics of AS may be ideal for you, in the right environment. If you are involved in work, programming, or teaching, your neurotypical fellow workers will share a number of these characteristics. Even the cliché, 'Things carried to extremes are always bad' doesn't apply to some tasks in modern-day work. Thoroughness and per-severation are valued assets in many jobs. A surprisingly high percentage of workers in the computer and information science field are somewhere on the autistic spectrum. The same tends to be true in library science, or any field that requires cataloguing, exquisite attention to detail, and great thoroughness. 'Number crunchers' such as insurance actuaries and accountants come to mind. University teaching abounds with odd, highly intelligent persons with extraor-dinary knowledge in exotic fields. Mathematics, computer science, many of the traditional sciences and other fields identified with eccentric lone thinkers make perfect havens for higher functioning individuals with AS. The very environment of higher education can act as a shelter and shield for highly educated people with rather primitive social skills. Here our competence is rarely challenged, and our peccadilloes are often overlooked. Where we often do badly is with the 'politics' of such workplaces. Even in less rarified employment, because many of us do so badly in the area of social skills, the idea of being a department head, supervisor, manager, or team leader may not seem particularly attractive. To some of us, it is downright scary.

In the business world, think what employee indifference to detail would mean in a commercial art studio or in a film studio specializing in animated characters. The same is true with the publishing and editing field. Think how dangerous lazy eyes are in a medical laboratory, or in a laboratory where workers check slides and samples all day. Even in highly automated environments, attention to detail is critical employee value. This characteristic in such jobs is exactly what is needed even though in other work and social settings it can be very exasperating.

CHAPTER 7

Personal Tools and Strategies

From early infancy we develop ways to survive in the world. We are still doing so. Think of these as tools in a toolbox. Some of the tools our parents gave us, some we fashioned on our own. Some we put together with others such as family members, teachers, therapists, mentors and acquaintances. Like all tools, our tools can get out of date or shopworn. Some lurk in the bottom of our toolbox, like that one tool we need for a very special situation. Some do not work any more, or have been lost. Some do not work, but we hold onto them for dear life anyway.

If you are going to write your employment biography, there are instructions in Part 2 on how to identify these tools, recall their use in your work, and assess their current and future value to you. If you are an adult reader, reviewing these tools may be a first time experience for you. As an adult, chances are you've had few of the medical, educational and other support services now available to children with HFA/AS in the public schools. You may have hacked through what you thought was your private jungle with little assistance from others, using a dull machete. You may still be in the jungle. By looking back, you can see the path you cleared. As in some jungles, however, that path behind you may have become quickly overgrown and not cleared for the next traveler behind you. With your additional understanding about yourself you may be able to keep that path clear for other sojourners if you are a parent, a teacher, or touch in any way the lives of others with AS.

With advances in learning theory, individually tailored services and technical assistance, many children who were once dismissed as impossible to teach or control have become participants in society. In K-12, the environment is supposed to change to accommodate the needs of disabled students. In the best school systems, physical and pedagogical changes have altered the picture for disabled students. They are on the path to becoming competent adults with fulfilling lives, a prospect unimagined just a decade ago. The possibilities for children in these systems appear very bright. However, the picture is not the same for children in bad school systems, and there are many such systems.

All children grow up. Disabled adults with hidden disabilities and cognitive challenges then face the full impact of ignorance and prejudice in the greater society. Architectural barrier removal, better ergonomic work conditions, improved lighting and ventilation, and increased safety awareness are benefits that affect all workers, disabled and able. The changes aren't just cosmetic. Along with the changes in the structure of the workplace and public places has come a slow change in the public perception of the challenges for impaired children and adults.

On first impression, we aren't impaired. From childhood, on second and subsequent impressions, we were and are. We know it, and a lot of people know it. The purpose of the exercise in Part 3 of this book is to help you discover your own tools, survival strategies and techniques. You will see what you have done, when you did it, *how* you did it, how you changed your techniques, and what new tools you need to fashion in a changing world so you can continue not simply to survive but to grow.

Like your assets – interests, skills and talents – your tools are actual or potential selling points as you market yourself in the world of work.

Marketing: Another adult job

Once you learn more about yourself as a worker, you can think of yourself as someone more than just a person hired by others. A list of our strengths suggests that while many of us may not be good in highly social settings, we can function, and do so successfully, in small businesses, and even start our own. With enough professional training and education, some of us have done just that. The two scenarios I outline below are intended to illustrate that the world of work is the world of business, whether we work for others or for ourselves. For those of us not able to work in the traditional sense, volunteer involvement in pursuit of our interests, or just to stay connected with the rest of the human race, may be essential to our mental health.

Two businesses

Imagine two kinds of businesses: The first is a second-hand ('thrift') store, and the second a new car dealership. Imagine further that their owners make good livings from their businesses. They are successful. What are some of the reasons for their success?

First, they know their product. For the second-hand storeowner, buying and selling previously owned merchandise is part 'art' and all business. The 'art' part is where the owner takes a chance with an article whose value she is not exactly sure of, but feels will sell at a profit. The business part is where the same owner knows her customer base, knows how to price her goods, and knows that there is a buyer out there. Second, she's studied the market. She's set up shop in the right location. Her prices are good, and if her wares are a cut above average she can charge 'top' prices for some items, because the quality of goods has given her store a good reputation.

Third, people don't just buy 'things'. They buy value. The difference between a item in shoddy condition in a bad store with poor quality merchandise with a high price, and the same merchandise with a higher price in a better store, is all about 'value' and the image of its worth in the mind of the buyer. There is a strong intangible operating here. The storeowner feels great about her business. She works hard to please her customers. She hires good sales people who don't give people a bad time when they return items that disappoint them. If customers are taken care of well, they return again and again. When the economy turns sour, her business will continue to thrive even though she has to make some 'cuts'. Nevertheless, she has good business sense. She never cuts what sells, and what sells is customer service and her passion as a businessperson.

Now think of the new car dealer. There is strong competition out there for the same car, and most of it is driven by price. Buyers aren't dumb. For big-ticket items, price is often very high on their list. Down the street is a second dealer selling the same car at the same price. That dealer has some sales-people who could as easily sell shoelaces as they could sell a forty thousand dollar sports utility vehicle. The dealer may have other salespeople who know everything about their cars. However, that dealer doesn't treat his salespeople very well. He has a very high staff turnover. You can tell. When a salesperson comes out to greet you, you just know that he or she is desperate to sell you a car. Everything about that salesperson tells you that. Maybe you feel pestered or badgered. Maybe the salesperson has sized you up in a split second and turns away knowing that you haven't come in to buy today, but just to 'shop'. Maybe all the salespeople are all trained to make snap judgments about customers. They do so on the basis of how the customer dresses, or the kind of car they arrive in. They can make you a great price. They may even have exactly the car you want, but you turn away and leave. Something isn't right. The cars are all lined up in the lot and the showroom looks great. Everyone has some kind of a smile on his or her face. Yet something is not right. It's an intangible thing. Maybe you understand; maybe you don't. What probably caused you to leave is a feeling that the salespeople don't feel very good about themselves as salespeople or as persons in general.

The competitor up the block has the same cars. He treats his salespeople well. Some of them have been with him since he opened, twenty, maybe thirty years ago. The salespersons seem to have definite personalities. They like their work, and they like 'working' with customers as well as selling to them. Their boss has allowed them to be 'who they are'. Because they know who they are, they are more observant about who you are. They welcome you and allow you the time and space to tell them who you are. In a way, they are selling themselves to you, but you don't feel the same kind of pressure you experienced three blocks down the street.

These people also know their product, but their primary aim as salespeople is to know you. That's how they convince you to buy the car. They have a big bag of tricks, survival techniques and things that work. They know how to choose the right tool to move you. They know when to put on the pressure, and when to back down. They 'read you' and your whole situation well.

One other thing about the dealers involved in this story. The owner down the block probably doesn't like himself very much. He may have all the trappings of success, but he may not be happy. Maybe he works a lot in his office or walks around his operation all the time because things aren't going well for him at home. Maybe he tinkers with this part of his business and that part of his business to fine-tune it. But he really doesn't 'get it'. In an extended lean time, he may go out of business.

The dealer you just bought your car from is more than likely a decent kind of guy. He likes himself, and others like him. He's serious about his business, but he loves it, so his love of the business – hard work to the other dealer – keeps him refreshed and open to new ideas. He may work just as hard as the other dealer, but there is a qualitative difference to his approach to business.

You buy your car from this dealer.

Selling yourself

People who know about themselves and who like who they are do a better job of selling themselves. Just as with the selling of merchandise – whether it is a used lamp or a new car – successful survivors in the business world have survival skills that they don't use only when they are desperate. At times when things are going OK, they use tools and strategies that prepare them for new challenges. They are careful and methodical about what they do in their everyday work. Of equal importance is how they go about doing it. The job of finding, retaining, and succeeding in work is more about selling than you'd think. With rapid changes in the job market and the economy, workers have to be flexible and good learners, and they have to be able to perform. By the time you complete your employment biography, you will know your selling points. You should have a good understanding of the positive parts of every experience in your three representative jobs. You should be able to speak about yourself in an authoritative, self-assured manner not possible before you undertook this serious study of your adult relationship with the world of work.

CHAPTER 8

My Wish List

Up to this point, this book has focused on issues influencing your past and the present. In this chapter we look at the future. If you intend to write your employment biography, return to this chapter after you have finished all but the last section of the workbook.

Worry worry worry

One kind of stress in our lives won't go away. It's called 'worrying about the future'. All of us, AS, autistic cousins and NTs, are subject to it. You can deal with worry a number of ways. The first is to let it rule your life. We're experts at that already, so perhaps more worry isn't the answer. We could also let our worry ruin the lives of others. Some of us are also good at that, so maybe that isn't too good an idea. Worry shortens lives just like depression. The two phenomena are related. Intelligent use of medication – natural or prescribed – is one way to tackle anxiety and worry. Combined with meaningful work, good diet, exercise, and more time with people (or pets) you like, there is a way to get a handle on it.

You can also harness the energy you spend on ruminating about things. It's called planning. Intelligent planning takes hard thinking and hard work. A lot of it isn't armchair work, either. Planning isn't a strong suit for most of us. This is one area where we should not only ask for help, we should demand it. Just having someone tell us to 'get organized' doesn't accomplish a thing for most of us. We must be shown how. Some of us have been shown how, but maybe we've forgotten. If we were lucky enough to have a good transition experience out of high school into adulthood, good planning played a big part in our success. Each of our accomplishments to which we can point with pride as adults also involved planning. Maybe we didn't think of it at the time, but in order to get to C from A, most folks pass B along the way. Sometimes we skip steps, but not very often. In making those steps concrete, in carefully reviewing the successful process we use to get where we are, we already have some very useful planning information at our fingertips. If you use the workbook as a guide to your employment history, your answers to questions asking you how you learn and work, and prompting you to look for connections between events, behaviors, and outcomes all provide useful planning data.

Most of us think that with the passage of time, doors close. Sometimes they do. We know that certain parts of our past are best left behind us. Recall the story of the incompetent managers and the good managers from the chapter on learning and work styles. There, the past wasn't really behind them. How they chose to use it was all-important. Without understanding where you have been, you may have trouble figuring out where you are now. You will definitely have trouble planning for the future. In thinking of the future, we don't merely 'form' a plan. We 'inform' a plan. A plan doesn't start from scratch. It has a history. We can bring the tough lessons and positive accomplishments and knowledge of our potential to bear in considering our future options. With your employment history, you already have a foundation for the future.

Imagine your foundation to be like the foundation of a building. Workmen dig a hole and remove dirt to construct forms and pour cement. Usually, they don't remove all the dirt from the construction site. If they did, the foundation, standing by itself, would be weak. After the foundation cures, dirt plus other more stable material is packed against the outside as backfill. Backfill keeps the foundation from buckling outwards.

In some societies where Portland cement and other expensive materials are not available, foundations are made of straw and other common materials, like clay. Workmen take dried or baked blocks of this material and use it as basic construction material for the building. Using natural materials found in the surrounding environment is a sound way to change a landscape. For those of us satisfied with the general quality of our 'material', we may not have to import expensive materials build our future. If we don't need high tech to accomplish sound goals we set for ourselves, why think of using it? Think simple.

Resistance

In the many agencies we turn to for guidance as adults, we don't seem to get anywhere, do we? We interact with professionals trained in 'case management'. They manipulate people and manage their lives. If we walk in with the idea of putting ourselves at the center of the planning process and collaborating with a professional to design our future, this may be a substantial challenge to some professionals' self-concepts. Major sources of resistance to our ideas about our own future are agency professionals who for years have 'talked' client independence but 'walked' dependence. For countless adults with AS, our counselors and case managers continue to tell us how much 'progress' we've made. Then there is a pause, followed by a 'but'. In the next few minutes they gently remind us about what we can't accomplish, of why we are not quite ready for the next step, or why our cases must be closed. Maybe we are ready for the next step, in which case they turn us over to contract job developers. Job developers are given so much agency money and so much time to find us a good job match for us. Job development agencies are numbers-driven. Reimbursement to the agency is based on the number of successful placements they make. In cruder terms, this translates to 'how many clients they can turn over'. Many counselors and job developers tantalize us with terms like 'training' and 'work assessments'. Training for what? For many of us, a dumbed-down job. Any job. We are placed. We remain at the job for 90 days. A successful placement. Maybe the job developer or the case manager 'made the numbers' for the month. Case closed.

Powerful words these: 'barriers', 'limitations', 'deficits', 'challenges'. Maybe the professionals don't use these words in the office when we are there. They come up all the time in other contexts. These words are the common currency of hallway conversations and staffing about us. Some of us find out 'what really is going on' by requesting to see our files. We see these terms in case notes, progress notes, and evaluations. Those notes reflect the real language spoken in many agencies. If these professionals were the only source of the 'truth' about us, we could continue to believe them.

They aren't, and now you know where some of the truth can come from: yourself.

If you encounter resistance to your plans and insistence on theirs, leave. It's OK to walk out. Some of them count on your leaving. They can't serve you because they don't understand your issues. Eventually, they'll take action that accomplishes the same thing as your leaving. They'll close your case. 'Too tough a client.' 'Not cooperative.' 'Resists direction.' 'Not on task.' It isn't going to happen there.

When you encounter this, don't try to reform the agency or the professional. Your efforts will be like trying to turn an ocean barge around in its own length in rough seas. One would think that because many of these agencies hire disabled persons, they could do a better job. Don't bet on it. Remember, disabled people are people first. And a lot of these people 'don't get it'. Being disabled in some agencies may only mean that they have a job. Helping your counselor or the agency 'get it' shouldn't be your crusade until and unless you get your own act together. Going on such a crusade while you are planning for your future may distract you from your real business: getting on with your life.

Person-centered planning

There is one kind of counseling and planning that rejects 'people management'.

Person-centered planning is both a planning and a counseling technique. It assumes that our wishes and dreams are what drive us and provide meaning to our lives. This is a simple enough concept. However, this notion shakes the very foundation of what many adult helping services have done for the past 90 years. In this respect, it is a radical planning paradigm. I urge you to seek it out and make it yours.

The one thing I urge upon all AS readers to this book, whether you intend to write your employment biography or not, is to consider person-centered planning. This is a specialized technique used with increasing frequency in rehabilitation, transition counseling, and the career planning process heavily subsided by the US federal government at all US Department of Labor funded 'One Stop' employment centers. There, a variety of services for all persons seeking employment are located under one roof. If you live in parts of the US where the One Stops are new, there is a strong chance that many persons staffing the centers are just going through the motions and it's business as usual. I don't say this to disparage all One Stops. The idea is excellent. Employment specialists simply have not always been given enough time and training before many One Stops opened. The test will be in the outcome, especially the outcome for 'people like us'. Lack of staff readiness in many One

Stops just happens to be the reality for now. I hope that with the passage of time things will improve.

Even though there is a shortage of person-centered planners, this situation shouldn't stop you from asking for person-centered planning services. Supply will follow demand – our demand. Our neurobiolgical condition is defined as one where we have substantial deficits in area of executive functioning. Substitute 'executive function' for planning, and there you have it: our nemesis. For most of us, even us very high functioning folks, this is our demon. Now that we've met it, it's time to deal with it.

Person-centered planners can be found in counseling departments at universities. They can be found in counseling education departments of schools of education. You can find them at regional training centers that contract with the US Department of Education, Rehabilitation Services Administration to train vocational rehabilitation counselors in your state. The United Cerebral Palsy Association in the US is a major mover and shaker with this approach in counseling. Other disability organizations may have similar counseling emphases.

There is one other source. There are private person-centered planners, and some are the best folks in the business. Most likely, insurance will not pay for their services. Agencies like vocational rehabilitation (VR) might. However, rather than struggle with VR over payment, remember my advice above: walk away from the naysayers and take charge of your life. Person-centered planners' fees are steep but not unreasonable. Consider two things. First, their training may have been lengthy and expensive. Second, we are very difficult folks to work with. It's a source of perverse pride with some of us, but there, I've said it. It's true. Some of us are so vigilant and defensive in our dealings with others that we simply won't let anybody 'in'. We've had it with invasive psychiatry and therapy and people poking and prodding us for our 'feelings'. As a precondition of working with them, they've set trust as an absolute requirement. Many of us don't trust others. That's also a known diagnostic trait. Why should they insist that we trust them before they even start to work with us? If we don't trust another person, how about working on our own self-trust? They can help us do that first.

When AS children learn – and they must be trained – to trust themselves, they can then start to trust others. They learn to distinguish between their own needs and the needs of others. Learning this takes a lot of work, but with adults, learning to know the difference between our agenda and that of another person is possible. In fact, most of us have learned it. We don't practice our understanding very well, but that's a different issue. Good person-centered planners don't have 'agendas' except in the general sense of wanting to move the personal planning process forward. You don't have to 'let them in'. You have to 'let yourself out'. Planners are not interested in playing mind games with you, so if you love to play mind games, forget the advice of this chapter until you decide which is more important – 'winning' – or getting on with your life.

Person-centered planners have a well-regarded technique, and that technique is to reflect your own aspirations back to you. This helps you test the strength of your convictions and the wisdom of the steps you take. If you don't like being confronted with your own evasive tricks or if you are uncomfortable with people who call you on your habits and thoughts that sabotage your progress, you aren't ready for this work. Person-centered planning is not just one more game. It is for real, and like cognitive behavioral therapy, it is hard work. If you decide to take it on, be prepared to face yourself in the mirror daily and question your ideas about the future. You are much more in charge of your future than anyone else. Up to now, you just haven't thought of things this way.

Three different scenarios

The start

Time doesn't stop. Our lives actually move faster than we think. If you are a young person at the beginning of the path to work, you have your whole life ahead of you. If you navigated special education and learned meaningful adult skills supportive of your independence, you are several steps of those who haven't fully benefited from what the special education system can offer. I hope that in leaving that system and entering the world of adulthood that you've learned to focus on your abilities and skills. Your success in selling yourself to an employer will depend upon the degree of fit between those assets and the employer's needs. If you are new to work, your value lies in your potential, not necessarily what you know about the job when you first start.

Somewhere in between, working for others

Most workers think of themselves as working for others. Doing anything 'with' others or in their presence is a challenge for people with Asperger Syndrome. Some of us have gotten quite good at it, while others of us show the strain by becoming virtual basket cases at the end of each work day. There is value in assessing the impact of AS on your work life by completing your own employment biography. Stress is impossible to eliminate, but your employment story can reduce your stress by providing you with knowledge about yourself. If you think of yourself as a person who works for others, self-knowledge gives you a good start to deal with present and future employment situations. Your most valuable assets are self-knowledge, your skill base, and how you demonstrate a willingness to learn. With knowledge you are better prepared to change direction. You can keep your good work habits, improve ones that need tuning up, and approach your next job with confidence.

Going it alone

If you are in the middle or a mature period of your work life, you may have less time but more opportunities open to you. From your experience as a worker, you know what could be done, made, acted upon, and changed in your former and current work setting to make a difference for others and yourself. This is what I refer to when I mention options. Many 'former employees' start their own businesses, or market themselves as 'fixers' or troubleshooters in businesses they are familiar with. Their skills are highly valued. They simply weren't appreciated as workers where they were employed so they quit and start their own business. Maybe they are encouraged by someone in that line of business to start off on their own. Some employers are willing to have outsiders come in and correct problems in their businesses. When a company is in trouble, some employers know they've gotten too close to things to see what has gone wrong. They realize they have too much of a personal stake in an unsupportable project, process, or product. They look around for consultants and technicians to help them get their businesses back on track. Performing such work takes great tact, and we know that tact is something we lack.

Rather than abandoning the idea of being a fixer, some of us have found bosses or other 'front people' to negotiate the details of our entry into these workplaces. They pave the way for us. That's what they are good at. Their advance work isolates us from employees or owners inside the business bent on sabotaging our work. In the world of information services and computer administration, technicians knowledgeable about the inner workings of a troubled system are shielded from cantankerous employees in a number of ways. Some 'techies' work at night or during hours others aren't around to interfere with their work. Some of them can't be paged, called, or distracted from their work, and everyone knows why: interruptions from such important work cost the company money, and they were hired to save the company money. Others train the business employees to become less dependent on techies and more knowledgeable themselves. Just as we benefited from one-on-one training, so we know many of the tricks that helped us learn. We can teach others using the same methods that worked for us.

Rather than having a boss, some of us become independent businesspersons or contract consultants. Since we tend to be solo operators anyway, we can play to our strengths as lone wolves. If we are good enough at what we do, we can plan for some of the unpleasant details of running the business to be handled by others. Book keepers, accountants, secretarial services, receptionists or others can perform many of our 'executive functions' without taking over our lives. We needn't necessarily use our own money for such ventures. Even if we draw some kind of disability benefits, public policy is shifting to support these kinds of entrepreneurial ventures. More foundations and funding sources are funding small businesses with micro-loans. Loans must be paid back, but the source of the money is usually close to us in our own communities. When we take the route of becoming independent business people, we can get training and start up support. Money for such purposes can be included in large and small venture capital loans.

These are not pie in the sky possibilities. Depending on our persistence, they can become real, but they take hard work. And perseverance. Perseverance is not the same as perseverative thinking for which we are well known. But just as we can apply single-minded thinking to our interests, so too we can hook this same neurobiological strength to planning for and accomplishing the steps essential to our long-term welfare.

PART 2

Workbook Instructions

Introduction

If you followed directions in Part 1, Chapter 1 'Three Jobs', you have already begun work necessary to complete your employment biography. You listed all your jobs, and then chose three jobs representative of three periods of your work life.

Questions and answers

'I have had fewer than three jobs. Will this book work for me?'

Of course it will. You might have held fewer than three jobs. Regardless of the number, they have meaning to you. Many persons have unpaid volunteer experience. That counts as well.

'What if I haven't worked at all?'

Even if you have never worked for pay, you have 'worked' in the sense that you have contributed to your family or school life. Even if you've never worked for pay, the questions in this book explore the world of work in a very thorough way. The author of this book assumes you know something about your own Asperger Syndrome and the impact that AS has had on your life. By answering the questions in the workbook you will gain a broader understanding of the issues of adult life and adult work. If you are a secondary school student, these questions may be of value to your parents and counselors as they work with you to plan your future and prepare you for adult responsibilities.

Even non-working adults have work-like responsibilities. In order to remain eligible for many kinds of assistance, adults must demonstrate that they can understand and follow the rules of agencies and others assisting them. How you learn those rules, how you demonstrate your understanding, and how you relate to others who employ these rules is 'work'. Many of the questions in this book relate to rules and responsibilities.

Knowing that the rest of their age peers are working, most non-working adults do not enjoy unemployment or underemployment. Whether we work or not, our work status defines us and contributes to how others see us. Even if it is difficult to be gainfully employed, many disabled adults contribute time as volunteers. If you volunteer your time, many questions in this book can apply to your volunteer experience. Volunteer work can often lead to paid work.

'How should I handle the task of actually writing?'

Any way that works for you. See the suggestions below.

In the instructions below and for the rest of this workbook, when I mention 'word processor' I mean either a computer word processor, a word-processing typewriter, a regular typewriter, or handwriting.

A few suggestions:

- You could answer the questions on one or two pages at a time in this workbook and then turn to your word processor and write your sentences and paragraph responses.

- You could time yourself [see the clock on the worktop in each illustration below] and decide that at the end of a certain period of time you will stop marking or writing your responses in this workbook and turn to your word processor to compose sentences and paragraphs.

- You could decide to make it through a certain number of questions and then start writing your composition.

There are other ways of handling the task of writing. Whatever means you choose, for each work session allow yourself enough time to actually write something. If you delay the process of composing for too long, you will not have a sense of making progress even though you mark your responses and write short answers for some questions. Be kind to yourself. Have your composed sentences and paragraphs in the form of written pages to be your 'reward' at the end of each work session.

'Why are these directions so complicated? Can't I just finish answering all the questions about each job before I move onto the second job?'

You could, but what you end up with will not be very useful. If you follow the directions for entering your answers, you will notice that you are working through the three jobs in stages.

Parts of this workbook ask you the same questions three times. Each set of questions refers to a different job you chose for an early, middle and late period of work. There is a logical reason why you should complete your written work for one aspect of each job before you move on to the next aspect. Working this way will help you focus on completing a single writing task at one time. It is important that you reflect carefully on the similarities and differences in your answers about each job. When you answer the same questions about the next job, your answers might be different. If they are, when you reflect on the differences you can track your personal development. If the subject area is an important one to you, writing about your change (if any) gives you information useful for making decisions about that area in your life.

'Should I answer the questions in the order they are written?'

Yes. I tried to organize questions around clusters of topics. Organizing your thoughts about a job in a topic paragraph can keep them 'corralled' without making them seem isolated and unconnected. By disciplining yourself to stick to a single topic, you can find that topic when you compare your reflections about it for each of your three jobs. Try to keep your answers clustered around a single topic but don't become obsessed about neatness of thought. Creative writing is never perfectly 'clean' or logical, except to the thinker, and your employment autobiography is a 'think piece' for you. The only difference between your autobiography and a strictly private piece of writing is that when you read your writing out loud – perhaps to another person – it should make sense and have some flow to it. It shouldn't read like a completely scattered collection of unrelated thoughts. This is especially so if you are working with a counselor helping you to sort out matters relating to work.

If you answer the questions in the exact order in which they appear, your thoughts may or may not flow smoothly. Every person thinks differently. As you answer one question, you may think of other details that complete your thoughts. The connections between details are what make your autobiography unique.

Completing this employment autobiography is hard work. Because you describe different aspects of three jobs, the paperwork you generate describing them will grow as you complete each section of the workbook. Storing your written answers in a ring binder will help you keep your material in order in one place. If you enter your answers in the workbook, you might find it easier to make preliminary notes on separate paper. You may wish to keep these notes for future reference.

How to use this workbook to compose your AS employment biography

There are at least three ways to write a work history. The first is simply to write your answers in the workbook and refer to the instructions for each section. The second is to treat the workbook as a far more complex exercise that produces greater self-awareness and self-understanding. To arrive at advanced knowledge, you will do much more writing. At the end of the process you will have completed a written employment autobiography that is separate from the workbook. A third way – a compromise – would be to take your lengthier written answers and boil them down to language that fits the space limitations of the workbook.

Choose a method best suited to your needs, adapting the guidelines that follow below to your chosen approach.

Much of the workbook is divided into three sections. Each section is for one job, and follows the order of text chapters in Part 1. As you complete your written work for each section, you build your work biography. Your answers about your work history will be composed in three sets of written responses; one set each for an early job, a middle-period job, and a current or recent-period job.

In most sections of this workbook, you are asked three kinds of questions. One type of question requires a simple 'yes' or 'no' answer. Another type of question requires you to select one or more best answers among several choices.

Some of these questions have space for you to answer with 'other', and describe that choice briefly. A third kind of question is open-ended, a form that allows you to write an answer using entirely your own words. Some of the 'essay' questions require short, detailed answers. Other questions, appearing at the end of some of the sections ask you to reflect on all of the material you've written for that section. You can summarize your answers, detect and explore connections between them and make general statements about yourself.

Some writers have trouble getting started, or knowing where to start. To help you past writer's block, there are samples or examples at the end of most sections to get you started. They illustrate how you can convert your workbook responses into simple sentences, and then string your sentences together into a paragraph. As you think about your writing, don't worry about how neatly the sentences will fit. It might be that your paragraphs have sentences with choppy, short sentences. Your sentences may not flow smoothly. That is OK. Each sentence contains important information about the job. For the purpose of this kind of an autobiography, that is enough. This guide is not a manual on how to write a novel or even a good 'story'. Think of your answers as a personal report to yourself.

Supplies needed to write your work biography

Although you can write your answers in the workbook section of this book, you may find it convenient to use a computer or word processor for writing your employment history. You will not be able to write your employment biography without producing a printed product. If you use a computer, save your work frequently and print a copy of your work at the end of each work session. Do not rely on the automatic 'save' features of your word processor. If you work on a computer shared by other people, save your work in a different location on your hard drive than your word processor's normal save location. If you are using a Windows-based operating system, you may wish to put your folder on your screen desktop. In addition to storing your documents on the computer hard drive, you should always make a permanent backup copy of your own data on a floppy disc or similar, portable external media source. Remember to save your work to your backup location at regular intervals during each work session. Use a timer or an alarm with a bell to remind you to do this. Saving your work this way will protect you against loss if your computer crashes.

One last thing about computer storage. Floppy discs are not reliable, permanent media. The more you use the same floppy disc, the greater the likelihood that it may become unusable due to corrupted sectors. Make it a point to do a 'disc copy' to new floppy discs on a regular basis and throw away the old discs. They are so inexpensive that you can afford this extra measure of reliability.

Print your work at the end of each work session. With a printed document, you can visually track your own progress through this workbook. As you work on your material, temporarily store it in a manila folder that you place in a pocket of your ring binder. Once you are done with the material, replace it between the chapter dividers of your binder.

Use the same size of paper for printing all your work. Number your pages for each chapter that you complete, and start each succeeding chapter with page number one. Numbering your pages in this manner will save you the job of renumbering your entire biography every time you make changes within chapters. Title each chapter and consider it a separate word processing file. When you are done with writing the separate chapters of your employment history, you can combine your chapters into a single folder. If your work is written or typed, your ring binder then will contain your original composition all in one place.

Materials you should buy to organize your work

1. A ream of pre-punched ring-binder plain, unlined copy paper.

This paper is sold in any well-stocked office supply store. It usually costs more than a ream of the same weight and grade of un-punched copy paper. If you can't find this paper, go to a copy center and ask them to use their hole punch machine to drill a ream of copier grade paper. Make sure the holes match the rings on your binder. Use this paper in your printer when you print out your written work for each chapter.

2. A sturdy two-inch ring binder.

A cheap binder will disappoint you. You will be opening and closing the rings on your binder many times. Invest in a heavy duty one. The best binders use a 'D-ring' or leaver arch configuration, not a round ring configuration. In addition to being sturdy, they allow you to store more paper in the same size of binder and turn your pages easier. Look for a binder with pockets for loose papers on the insides of the front and back covers. Make two labels titled 'My Employment Biography'. Tape a label to the spine of the binder as well as onto the front.

3. A package of binder divider sheets.

These sheets are stiff, card-stock weight sheets of paper available in buff manila or colors. Look for binder dividers with tabs on them. You will need one to separate your chapters for easy access in the ring binder.

4. A package of colored tabs.

Many of your written chapters will contain sets of answers relating to each of your three jobs. Use the same color tab in your chapters to identify your writing for your early-period job, your middle-period job, and your later-period job. Some packages of colored tabs come with too few tabs of the same color. While you are at the stationery store, make sure you have enough tabs of the same color to work with all of your materials.

5. A dozen manila folders.

Some folders come with tabs on them. Don't buy the ones without tabs. Cut the tabs off. There is a good reason for doing this. They will then be smaller than a regular folder. You want them smaller so you can store them in your ring binder pockets.

This guide will instruct you to write answers to questions that require you to review and compare your earlier writings. You could flip back and forth between sections of your ring binder to do this if you have a good short-term memory. Many of us don't. We can't remember things we just did or viewed until we actually see them again, physically manipulate them or repeat them out loud. Instead of flipping back and forth, it may be easier for you to compare things when they are actually laid out side-by-side before you on a worktop or a desk. This is when the manila folders come in handy.

When you encounter questions asking you to review earlier answers, you can remove those pages from your binder and work with them 'loose' on your desktop. If you were to leave them lying around they could easily get intermixed with other loose sheets. At each point in this book where you are asked to reflect on your earlier work or compare your answers, there are illustrations showing you what you should have laid out before you on your worktop. When you are working with these loose sheets, use the folders temporarily to keep the pages in one place until you have finished consulting them. Between work sessions, if you need to work with loose pages in this way, always place your material in the folder. Then store your folder inside the cover pockets of your ring binder. Storing your work in the folder ensures that your uncompleted work can be found in the same place when you start your next work session.

Your desk top

If you want to write a complete employment biography, you will need to use all of the organizing materials listed above to answer the workbook questions. Even if you use a computer to record your answers in sentence and paragraph form, you must use a work surface large enough to accommodate this book, manila folders, a ring binder and your printed or handwritten pages. If you use a watch, timer or clock, place it on or above your work area.

For each workbook section there are illustrations depicting the likely appearance of your desktop. The illustrations may help in the physical organization of your work materials. Illustration 1.1 depicts all of the possible materials you could be using. It is unlikely your desktop will ever get this crowded.

Clockwise, from the upper left corner, are the following items:

- Written or printed pages, each tabbed to refer to one of your three jobs

- Binder dividers to be placed in your ring binder to separate each portion of the workbook

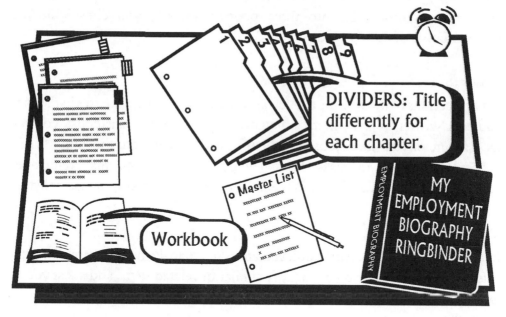

 = Early Period Job   = Middle Period Job   = Late Period Job

Illustration 1.1

- Your timer, watch or clock
- Your ring binder with inside storage pockets
- A master list
- This book, opened to Part 3 containing questions for you to answer.

If you choose to write a shorter biography or just to write in the workbook by itself, you will still need a work surface large enough to spread out your work when you start to compare answers across periods of your work life or when you are writing summaries.

Lists: Other tools you create and tools created for you

Your first list

You are nearly ready to start writing. Actually, you've already started. When you read the first chapter of Part 1, you were asked to write a list of all the jobs you've ever held. You turned to the first page of the workbook to do that. Then you divided those jobs into three periods. Finally, you chose one job representative of each period.

Master lists

In two sections of the workbook, you are asked to compose a 'master list'. Once you have written as many items as you can think of for the master list, you can look at one of your three jobs and identify which items from the long list fit a particular job and its tasks. In reviewing each job, you may remember additional items, and as you recall them, you can add them to your master list.

Other smaller lists

In other sections of the workbook you are asked to make lists that aren't master lists. These lists will help you identify similar or related items and assist you to write your observations and summaries of work experiences throughout your work life.

Lists by the author

The list of social skills found in Section 2 on social skills is a combination list and rating scale. The list of *Asperger Syndrome Characteristics* is a list you consult when answering questions about the effect your own features of AS have had upon your work. Another list is found in Section 8. The questions in that list can serve as an outline for making your personal plans.

Starting and finishing

How to get started

For many people, starting on a big project is difficult. Choose a quiet place and schedule time to do your work on a regular basis. Distractions and interruptions will delay your start or cause you to lose your train of thought. Tell others that this work is important to you and that you do not want to be disturbed while writing. Once you start, work in any manner comfortable for you. Some people find breaks helpful while others just charge along. Try to write quickly once you start, although if you are the kind of person who wants perfect grammar, spelling and punctuation as you work, honor those needs but don't let them bog you down to the point where you are reluctant to continue to write.

Consulting others

This is your work biography. There are no right or wrong answers. For some of the items you may need to consult diaries, journals or other personal documents. Do not ask others to 'verify' your experiences or impressions except to help you to recall the order of jobs you held or some of your job tasks. Your primary sources of information are your own experiences and perceptions. Except in one topic area, social skills, you should not rely on someone else's view of what happened. Asking others to help you write your autobiography is like asking them to provide information about the dreams you have at night. If others offer their help, politely decline it. This work biography is your own personal road map and navigational chart. In order to make the maximum use of it, you must totally own it.

About finishing

Some of us are never satisfied with what we write. Good writers often never are. But there comes a time when our 'editor' – whether it is yourself or another person – says, 'STOP ALREADY!' Listen to your editor. Don't criticize yourself for being less than perfect. You would never finish. Do not add to your work unless your addition materially affects the direction of your writing in a section of the workbook. There is always time for you to add material for your own benefit later, after you have started to use your employment biography. Remember that this biography is a personal tool, and consider it ready when you finish it. If you are always polishing a tool you will never use it.

When your employment biography is complete, you will have covered the topics below in the order in which they appear here.

1. Three jobs
2. Social skills
3. Learning and work styles
4. Interests, skills and talents
5. My work and Asperger Syndrome
6. Personal tools and strategies
7. Diagnosis, disclosure and self-advocacy
8. My wish list.

1. Three Jobs

The instructions for this part of the book all refer to identically titled sections in Part 3, the actual workbook. You are to answer the same questions about each of the jobs you chose as representative of your early, middle and late periods of work. An illustration in this section serves as a visual organizing guide for your work.

Take a manila folder, cut off its tab, and label it 'Jobs: Chapter one.' You will be using this folder many times. Each time you store your work in progress temporarily, loose sheets can be placed in this folder and stored in one of the inside pockets of your ring binder. If you use a word processor, open up three blank documents, and title each for your early, middle and late work periods. Print the pages. If you handwrite or type your employment biography, take three sheets of paper and title them in the same manner. Take out your packages of colored tabs and decide which color you will use to tab each period's written work. For example, all of your materials for the early job could be tabbed in red, while the middle period could be green, and the late period could be yellow. The color choice is up to you.

These three sheets are the cover sheets for the pages you compose with the answers pertaining to each of your jobs.

Before you begin answering questions in Section 1 of the workbook, thumb through the entire section quickly. There are two reasons why you should do this. The first is to get a sense of how much detail the questions cover. If many of the questions do not fit the first job you chose, that of your early work period, make another choice from your 'All my jobs' list that is more representative of the entire first period. Do the same for your middle-period job. Once you are comfortable with your choices, you should be able to answer most of the questions.

Even if your job is representative of that period, certain questions may not apply. As you consider each question, mark 'NA' for 'not applicable' in the answer area. Use this response only if the question really doesn't apply to the job at all. If you forget to write 'NA,' that might indicate that you overlooked the question. When to compose sentences and paragraphs, you will know that you considered the question because you chose to answer with an 'NA' response.

The second reason for thumbing through all of the questions is to familiarize yourself with how the answer from one question can affect your answer in the next question(s). Throughout the workbook, questions are clustered around topics. Those topics mirror the subject matter of the text materials at the beginning of the book. If you preview the questions in advance of writing about each one, you will perceive a flow from one topic to the next.

There are sample answers at the end of this section. They illustrate how you can convert your answer to each question into a simple sentence, and string your sentences together into paragraphs. You might want to glance at the examples before you turn to the questions in the workbook, but don't spend much time reading and worrying about how to write. Once you've finished the questions in the workbook and reach the 'essay' section parts, you can use the examples as guidelines. To keep yourself on track, you may wish to re-read some of the general instructions in this introduction.

The illustrations below and in the following sections are depictions of your worktop. Illustration 1.2 shows an answer page dealing with questions about your late period job. Note that answer pages from the earlier periods are placed in the manila folder at the upper left corner of the worktop. After questions relating to the last period are answered, you will be asked to take out your pages from the first two jobs and compare your answers. Your observations then become summary comments for this first topic.

If the illustrations found in these pages of instructions do not seem right for the way you work, try to 'visualize' your own picture of the writing process. One thing is important, however. Try to be consistent. Consistency is all a part of establishing a routine when you write. However, don't become a slave to consistency. If one method of working through this guide loses its effectiveness after a while, take a break from your work. When you come back, try another method.

One final tip before you begin: Unless a question asks you to describe changes in your job as you held it over time, answer each question as it applies to your overall experience of that job from beginning to end. You might feel uncomfortable answering a question that doesn't quite satisfy you. You might want to fret over and polish each answer.

Don't.

What you should describe is your 'journey' through a job. You don't have to stop to describe each pebble in the road, or each blade of grass along the way. You are composing an employment autobiography that will act like a road map. In reading it later you won't be interested in many of those small details. If you put them in now they will divert you from your real work. Stick to the main agenda. Concentrate on answering the questions as if someone was interviewing you and you want to keep their interest.

When answering the questions in this chapter where a blank appears in the question, choose the most appropriate answer from the choices appearing below the question. The choices of answer presented are not exhaustive. If none of the choices fits but the question still applies to the job, write your own answer. Only use this process with multiple choice questions with a blank line.

Do not 'customize' your answers in other multiple choice questions that force you to make a choice. Although these are not 'test questions,' they are clearly worded so that anyone later helping you with employment-related

▤ = Early Period Job   ▥ = Middle Period Job   ■ = Late Period Job

Illustration 1.2

counseling will understand the 'language' of the question. It is important that you use the same language by confining your answers to the choices in that question.

Caution about Question 13

Of all the questions regarding your work, Question 13 is the most complex. You will return to it several times as you work through the sections of the workbook. Two of its sub-topics refer to how you learned the tasks of your job and how you actually performed them. Do not answer those two questions during your work on this first 'go around'. Doing so will distract you from answering the other questions following Number 13. After you have reviewed your understanding of social skills and communication in the job in Section 2 of the workbook, you can return to Question 13 to answer the two learning and work-style questions.

Text examples

Here are two types of text examples you might consider when writing your own employment biography. The two examples are drawn from different questions about your three jobs. Those questions are numbered 1 through 73 in Part 3 in the first section of the workbook. The first example uses sentences that follow the actual wording of the questions very closely. If you wish to finish your written work quickly, consider using the first approach. The paragraphs aren't works of art, but they answer the questions, and they do work as a 'self-report'.

The second example is more literary. The writer has spent more time polishing his work, and the information contains some nuances missed in the first example. You decide which details are important, but keep in mind that the purpose of this workbook is for you to attain a better understanding of yourself by looking in depth at your work, and then moving from contemplation to action. Think of this whole exercise as the laying of a table for a good meal. To do that, you don't need to embroider doilies when a plain table cloth will do just as well.

EXAMPLE 1

This example is taken from Questions 1 through 9.

> My job title was 'cabinetmaker'. I learned about the opening from an employment office. I was hired mainly due to my experience and knowing the superintendent from previous visits. My work was inside, with full-time hours. That was what I wanted. I was paid an hourly wage and had full benefits. There was little chance of promotion. The reality was that once you were hired in a certain position, you stayed there. My pay was inadequate. My employer allowed me some accommodations for missing work.

Questions 28 to 33 refer to sensitivity and discomfort. Here are three sample paragraphs written in answer to those questions. Notice how the first sample describes the sensory environment. The second describes what the writer did to change things. The third describes what others did to change things.

> I worked in a noisy environment where my tasks included driving a forklift, operating a cardboard compactor, and some noisy portable power-tools. I wore earplugs which helped a bit in reducing my discomfort, but could not do those tasks all day. The strobe lights on the back of the forklifts hurt my eyes, but I couldn't avoid them unless I got to work in the office area, where I did all the computer entries for my department. I was also bothered by the whirling displays near the sales counters. In one location in the building, they hadn't changed the lights in a long time and the flickering drove me nuts.
>
> I managed to avoid the flickering lights by working in one corner of the area where the lights were still OK. There were some odors, especially those coming from the sign shop, but I asked them to keep the doors shut and the exhaust-fan running. Once one of the smells coming from a blue print machine made me so sick I nearly 'lost it' on my way to the restroom. I asked the clerk in the office to do all the blue print copying that had been left for me to do. She actually enjoyed the work, and I did anything she asked in return for the favor. When I was handling freight, they made me wear some uncomfortable scratchy gloves. I solved the problem by wearing some lightweight cotton gloves underneath. When I was really bothered by something I just walked away.
>
> Once I told the superintendent about the noisy compactor, and he shrugged and said that working in that area was part of my job description and that I'd better get used to it or find another job. A couple of people from the evening staff were helpful. They saw that I was really upset by the noise, and suggested I work in another part of the building after the supervisor left. Another evening worker told me that some new lighting was being installed in the area where the old lights were flickering. I had mentioned to her how nauseous the flickering made me feel, and she

arranged for me to work in the nursery building until the electricians had installed the new lights.

EXAMPLE 2

In the examples below, notice how the writer has opened up his paragraphs to explore and discuss his job. His paragraphs go beyond providing minimal information, and he has started to paint a broader picture. He also thumbed through some of the later chapters in the workbook and has started to make some connections between his version of AS and how it influenced his work. Here, the writer has answered Questions 28 to 33.

I had sensory challenges from the moment I arrived at work to quitting time. The noise level where I worked was often deafening (literally), objects were constantly being misplaced or relocated and the lighting was too weak. (It was the wrong type to reveal flaws and condition of the product.) I had to bring in my own work lights. The bulbs were expensive and my employer did not pay for the replacements. Over-spray and curing finishes from the finishing area made me physically nauseous. There was never enough room to maneuver without risking damage to raw or finished items. I was unable to reduce or eliminate the source of my discomfort although I did take to wearing earplugs nearly all the time.

Although I expressed my concerns about these conditions, the work itself, the placement of the workstations and the nature of the operations allowed no real sensory relief. Everyone 'suffered' under the same conditions.

When the overload of work combined with noise or frequent distractions and interruptions, I 'lost it' a lot. I was grumpy one minute, and fine the next. I guess no one really knew what my mood was until he or she actually checked in with me. I often didn't know myself.

The last sample of writing covers Questions 33 through 45. Note how all of the questions are answered, but here the writer is providing his impression of experiences.

This was a manufacturing operation run from the top down. For the most part, that meant that people had to stifle creativity and originality on the shop floor. There was strong emphasis on doing things by the book, literally. The problem was, they kept changing the book. No sooner did I understand one way of doing things when they imposed a change, often a very minor one. If I was stressed, it always seemed major to me, and I let 'them' know it. I got a reputation as a whiner and a critic. I wanted predictability in an unpredictable world. The longer I was there the harder it became for me to stifle a general sense of cynicism. The trouble was, I was not privately cynical. I trumpeted it.

Senior employees who had been there a long time took changes in stride, but they also expected others to read their minds. A lot of what established the good reputation of our product was stored in their heads, and some of them kept that information there until an event on the floor or a big, expensive mistake forced it out of them. In this environment, new employees were afraid to ask the senior employees every time they had a question.

We were fearful of the consequences, which were often expressions of exasperation and body language telling us, 'You should know that...I do.' Less experienced employees had to sneak their questions to slightly more experienced ones, and people were always being warned not to leave their work stations. Needless to say I always had questions and was always everywhere else in the shop other than in my work area. Overtime and other demands were announced with little forewarning, and workers having medical or routine family business to attend to felt generally disrespected for their private lives. Under many circumstances, grown adults were made by supervisors to feel like unruly, undisciplined children. Many new-hires quit rather than work under such conditions. I had to stay. I needed the steady work.

2. Social Skills

The instructions in this section refer to Question 74 in the workbook. The workbook section on social skills is composed of only one question, but the question has many parts. In marking your responses to the questions in the workbook, you are to report your awareness of the social rules in each of your jobs. While you could describe your understanding of those rules in comparison with other employees in that same setting, here you are asked to use the *assessments of others* of your social skills. In reporting their assessment, don't guess at what they thought or meant. Rely for your answer on what they actually said directly to you.

Their words to you reflected how they viewed your understanding of social rules and how you practiced your social skills through your words and actions towards them and others. In describing your skill level try to avoid self-criticism. Your answers depict your image not in your own mirror, but in the 'mirror' of others. Be an accurate and honest reporter. This may be difficult for you. If you misreport your own social skill level by being dishonest or not reporting the words of others, much of the value of writing your own employment biography will be lost.

Your answers should be an accurate reflection of the remarks others who were important to your hiring, retention, and advancement made to you about your social skills. On the other hand, you might weigh your answers differently if you include the casual remarks of people who didn't interact with you much. Casual remarks often reveal people's real feelings about their relationships and knowledge about you. Spur of the moment observations of supervisors and co-workers can affect the overall level of comfort you felt on a job. For example, you might have had a great boss but lousy co-workers. Day to day interaction with bad co-workers can override the benefit of having a good supervisor. Overall, the stress level in such a job is likely to be very high. Even if you are the only person feeling stressed out by others' remarks about you, you aren't the only person affected by those remarks. High stress affects the social environment of the workplace. When people are careless, disrespectful or inconsiderate towards one worker, the entire work environment suffers. Performance drops. While cliquishness and 'politics' are a normal part of any situation where more than two people are involved, a workplace can easily assume a toxic 'feel' to it when these dynamics are permitted to continue. I say 'permitted' because management sets the tone for a workplace. If managers don't care or contribute to the negativity of a workplace, they are the ones responsible for turning matters around.

In recording and reviewing your answers, you might be tempted to form a bleak overall impression of your social skill competence. Remember that two of the three jobs you have chosen for your autobiography are in your past. As for your last or most recent job, consider yourself a work in progress and a person capable of change. How you can reach a higher level of communication and social skills is something you will take up in the last chapters of your autobiography. You must travel the other paths of your personal discovery tour in the other sections of this workbook.

How to work with Question 74 in Part 3

To help you do this work, questions about your social skill understanding are presented as statements on a three-choice scale. There is a complete set of social skills questions for each of your three jobs. Unlike the first lengthy section of the workbook (Questions 1 through 73) where you may have chosen to write your sentences and paragraphs after answering a few questions at a time, do not start to write about your social skills for that job until you have gone through every question on the scale for that job. As you first mark your level of under-standing for each social skill on the scale, make your answer reflect your overall understanding of that skill during the entire period you held the job. Your 'mark' for each skill should be similar to a final grade mark at the end of a class. Doing this for each skill will help you form a complete picture about your overall skill level for that job. There is room at the end of the exercise for you to report your progress in attaining social skills or improving them at different times as you held the job. For the moment, just record your 'final score'.

▤ = Early Period Job ▥ = Middle Period Job ■ = Late Period Job

Illustration 2.1

After you have marked your answers for the early period job, take a page of paper and title it 'Social Skills'. This will be the first page of several pages you may compose describing your social skills for that job. Attach the same color of tab on the edge of the first sheet that you used for your early period job pages for your written answers to Questions 1 through 73. After you are done with the first period job, place your written material in a manila folder and proceed to your middle period and then to your late period jobs. As you start your written pages, remember to tab them with the same color of tab used for your answers for the same period for Questions 1–73.

Illustration 2.1 shows how your worktop should appear as you are in the middle of this operation.

Instructions and text examples for Chapter 2

The chapter on social skills in Part 1 of this book concludes with a question. The question relates to what others really meant when they talk with you about your social skills. For the purpose of answering the scaled items in Question 74 in Part 3, if you have to work hard to understanding what they meant, it is better for you to leave the question unanswered than take a wild guess. Mark these questions with a question mark ('?'). As you review all of your scale responses to write paragraphs about your social skills, note which ones you had no easy way of marking. Pay attention to those skills when asking yourself how important they may be for the job. Later on, you can make your own list of skills to learn more about. Your question mark responses indicate social skills you may need to work on.

Your answers should be an accurate reflection of the remarks others made to you about your social skills. Don't use 'wiggle words' which have different meanings in different contexts. Avoid words like 'kind of', 'perhaps', 'maybe' or phrases that could mean anything to anybody. Be clear and consistent with your use of words. Use precise words or phrases to describe your actual level of a social skill. If your text is full of vague words, you won't be able to identify which skills needed attention when people told you about them. Because you won't have a clear picture of your skill level, it will be hard to identify the skills you may need to acquire or improve now and for the future.

For each question, recall other people's words, and then summarize them through the filter of the three choices in the scale: 'good', 'poor' and 'none'. Use 'no' or 'not' as a grammatical substitute for 'none' where necessary. Some of your sentences may be choppy and short. That is OK. As you can see from examples below, you can write variations of 'no' and still leave the meaning clear.

Following your last paragraph of written answers for your first job, write a summary paragraph describing changes in your understanding of the social rules that you experienced during the course of the job. While some of your social skills may have remained at the same level others may have changed. Recall the level of your skills at the start of your job and compare that level to your skill level at the end of your job. Write about the job tasks, events or persons contributing to that difference. If conditions changed outside of the job, did those external changes have an impact on your social skill practices at work? Write about those 'outside factors' as well.

Follow this same process for your middle-period and late-period jobs.

Below are several paragraphs illustrating a way to convert your 'X's' to writing.

EXAMPLE TEXT ANSWERS DERIVED FROM 'X'S' ON THE SCALE

I had a poor understanding of the proper greeting and departure phrases, and appropriate gestures and body language. I had a good understanding of how to show respect to everyone, no matter their level.

I had trouble with not telling the whole truth. I was a poor judge of when to be frank and honest, and I could not tell social lies, or to make up stories just to entertain people. I told no factual lies.

EXAMPLE OF SUMMARY OF SKILL DEVELOPMENT PARAGRAPHS

When I first started the job, I was 'Mr. Questions'. I hadn't done a lot of the operations before which were required of the job. I was told there was no such thing as a stupid question, and to put it bluntly, I made a pest of myself asking too many questions. Finally, the programmer in the cubicle next to me pointed to a notebook on his desk and said he took notes a lot when he first started.

He gave the notebook to me, and I made files of notes. They covered some of the more advanced operations I knew I would be asked to perform. I wrote down any questions I had and made a point of saving up many of them before I asked for help. After going through my list of questions, I would bring a select list to staff conferences. I asked the other questions at lunch of my co-workers who liked to 'talk shop' during lunch. In my three-month review, my supervisor said she was relieved I had taken this initiative. She said that when I first started, other workers had come to her with concerns about my interrupting their work so often.

3. Learning and Work Styles

These instructions refer to Question 13 in the first section of the workbook. When you first answered Question 13, you were asked to skip the questions relating to how you learned the tasks of your job and how you performed them. Now is the time to return to these items.

Before you do, review the list of eight intelligences found in the Part 1 chapter on learning and work styles following the sub-title 'What you learn and how you learn it'. Re-reading the Gardner list may help you write your answers to Question 13. As with 'Social Skills', you are to complete your answers for the tasks of one job completely before moving to the next job.

Completing your employment biography section on your learning and your work style is a two-step operation. The first step involves your turning to the tasks of each job and writing brief answers in the workbook just about how you learned the tasks of the job and how you performed them. After you complete your workbook responses for all three jobs, there is a second step. The second step requires writing additional information on separate pages outside of the workbook.

You already determined whether each task was hard or easy, and whether you learned and performed all, part, or none of it. Under the task description, there are two spaces for a written response. The first item reads, 'What I did to learn the task'. Whether or not you found the task easy or hard to learn, answer the additional questions only about those you learned ('Y') or partially learned ('P'). Do not write any answers for tasks you did *not* learn. Start with the tasks you found easy to learn. If you pick apart the task, you will see that its mastery may have required learning in a certain sequence or series of steps. Try to recall them. Write a brief and specific answer describing what you actually did to learn the task. Do not write answers such as, 'It was just easy', or 'I had no trouble with it'. Instead, your answers should read something like this:

In order to learn X, I did L, M, and N.

You need not confine your answer to just three steps. Also, some tasks only require one learning step. Complete your answers for each 'Easy' task in the early-period job set. After you are done with the easy tasks, turn to the 'Hard' ones.

The last blank space for each task in Question 13 deals with how you work ('How I did the task'). After you write your brief answers about how you learned each task, describe how you performed that task. Then go on to the next task to describe your learning and your working process in the same way. As with the question above, be specific in your answers. A typical answer should look something like this:

In order to do X, I did O, P, and Q.

Next, turn to each task in the set you marked with an 'H' for hard to learn. Repeat the same steps you followed in the two paragraphs above. When you are finished with the early-period job period set, turn to Question 13 in the workbook for your middle-period job and repeat your short answer process. Once you finish with the middle-period job tasks, turn to your late-period section of the workbook and complete those short answers.

TWO SAMPLE ANSWERS

Here are two examples of workbook answers. They are examples only. Don't worry about style or doing a 'perfect' job. Do not spend a lot of time with each task. Write quickly.

Examples

13. Job Tasks and Responsibilities

TASK

(A) _Special production run_
machine set up and training for
other operators
_____
_____

Learning Difficulty

Hard (H) Easy (E)

Learned?

Yes (Y)   Partially (P)   No (N)

What I did to learn the task:

> I watched the operators over a two-day period, and made notes about their performance. Then I asked each operator about what they needed to feel safe doing the production setup. I watched my lead person train new employees with different levels of experience on another machine. I asked her for some tips, and she trained me on a machine new to me. I also watched her coach an operator who had been on that machine for a while, and observed her doing check-in and confirmation on each new task she taught.

How I did the task:

> I set up the machine with safety measures exceeding the needs of the most inexperienced operators. I divided the operators into two groups, an inexperienced group, and a partially experienced one. I had everyone watch while I took each inexperienced operator through an individual training. After that, I randomly assigned them to the operation, observed them once an hour, and reviewed the whole job progress at the end of each day. I did some fine tuning the following days until the job was done.

13. Job Tasks and Responsibilities

TASK

(B) _Quarterly full staff present-_
ation on future work projections
for my unit _____
_____
_____

Learning Difficulty

Hard (H)   Easy (E)

Learned?

Yes (Y)   Partially (P)   No (N)

What I did to learn the task:

I was new to management-level work. I contacted the company training manager and he showed me three videos. The first one showed me all kinds of aids to use. The second one showed me how to do an outline for a presentation. The third one was a start-and-stop video, where the training manager actually videotaped me doing parts of the presentation, we reviewed it together, started the video for the next step, stopped it and taped me during the next part of the presentation, and so on. After the video was done, I did a taped presentation from start to finish, and we reviewed it. I contacted my old supervisor and did the whole ten-minute presentation for him. He gave me additional tips for things that would work well in our section.

How I did the task:

My first presentation was kind of rocky. I had too many confusing graphs, but the prototypes I brought were very useful. I thought I had prepared well for the questions, but I muffed that part. This was something I didn't ask about during the training. I guess the training manager assumed I could handle questions, and so did my former supervisor. The next presentation went better, but before I had a third chance, I was transferred to another project group. I didn't have any more chances to do presentations after that.

Converting workbook responses to your biography

- *If you are writing the 'long version' of your employment biography, follow the instructions below.*

- *If you are writing an abbreviated version, read the questions relating to each issue raised in the following pages and compose abbreviated responses. Write your answers in whatever form works best for you and key your written materials to the 'Learning and Work Style' section of the workbook.*

To write an extended evaluation of your learning and work styles, you will have to do some additional desktop organizing. You will first be writing about one job at a time, and finally writing a summary of your learning and work styles from a review of all three of your jobs.

Refer to Illustration 3.1, below. It depicts the materials you will use for this extended exercise.

▤ = Early Period Job   ▥ = Middle Period Job   ▮ = Late Period Job

Illustration 3.1

Take a manila folder and label it: 'Learning and Work Styles'. Place your written work for this section in it until you complete all of your writing for this section. Take out a blank piece of paper or open a new document in your word processor. Title your page 'Learning and Work Styles'. On the upper right hand corner, identify the job by using the words 'early', 'middle' or 'late', as appropriate. As you complete your written material for each job, attach the tab of the color you earlier chose to identify your first, middle, or late period job writing for each chapter. Place the tab on the first the first page for that job so that you can easily locate it later. After you have finished writing about your learning and work styles for each job, you are asked to further evaluate them by looking for patterns or consistencies shared by more than one job. To make that work easier, you should write your descriptive paragraphs following the order of the tasks as you listed them.

Start by selecting each of the tasks that you marked with an 'E' for easy to learn. Even though you covered some of this information when answering Question 13 in Section 1 of the workbook, there is a reason for writing this information down a second time. Describe the tasks using the same words you wrote in your workbook entry. For each task you marked as easy to learn, indicate whether you learned it completely or partially. If you wrote complete sentence responses on the workbook pages, copy the entries just as you wrote them. For each task, if there is more you want to add about how you learned the task and how you actually performed it, write that information in your paragraphs.

Once you finish writing about each easy task for the job, turn to those tasks you found hard to learn, but that you did learn either completely or partially. Repeat the same writing process for these hard to learn tasks as you followed above.

Finally, before you move on to the next job, write about those tasks you did not learn. Describe them completely. You have confirmed that you didn't learn some tasks. Now is the time to start thinking about why.

Try to recall times prior to being employed in that job when the same issues came up for you. Remember back to any learning challenges you might have had in school. Think whether the tasks you didn't learn at work were similar to the tasks you found difficult or impossible to master as a student. If the tasks you didn't learn were critical to that job, you can begin to see how jobs with such tasks may have been unsuitable for you at that time. Don't beat yourself up about this knowledge. Regardless of how painful it may be to recall this information, it is important information for you to use in assessing your present job or inquiring about future ones.

Before moving on to writing about the next job, take some time to review all of your workbook answers from Questions 1 through 73. Then look at the level of social skills you had in your answers about the same job in Section 2 of the workbook at Question 74. Are there conditions of the job that you identified earlier that blocked learning opportunities for you? Were there conditions that enhanced your learning of tasks? Jot down any thoughts that arise in this informal review, and hold them for discussion at the end of this chapter. Print your material, tab the first page with the color you chose for your first job, and place your written work in your ring binder.

Repeat this process for the middle period job and your late period job. Tab the first page with the right color tab, and place your written paragraphs in the binder.

Writing a summary of your style of learning and working

You will need a clear worktop to accomplish this next task. Once you complete your written answers for all three jobs, take two clean sheets of paper, or open up two computer files. Title one sheet or file, 'How I Learn'. Title the second, 'How I Work'. Each of these documents will become final pages to chapter three of your employment biography. These pages are your summaries.

Refer to Illustration 3.2 below. It depicts the organization of materials on your worktop. At the upper left hand corner of the worktop are tabbed bundles of documents. These are your observations, connections, and conclusions about your learning and working processes for each job. Note that each bundle is color-tabbed for a job period. In the middle of your worktop are your summaries.

To write summaries of your over all styles of learning and working, you will need to compare your styles for all three jobs. To do that, you may find it helpful to spread material out on the table so that you can shuffle quickly back and forth between your jobs. Writing your summary paragraphs for this chapter may take some time.

You have two sources of information to help you with your summary of your personal learning and working style. The first source is your responses to the parts of Question 13. These are your 'short answers'. You just finished that

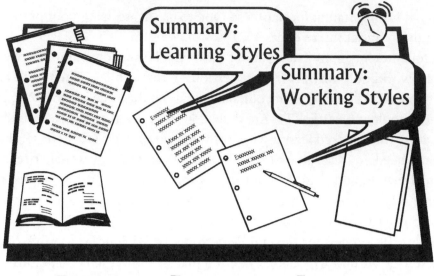

= Early Period Job   = Middle Period Job   = Late Period Job

Illustration 3.2

work in the workbook. You wrote about how you learned and how you worked for each task. The second source is the expanded writing you just completed. You color-tabbed this writing.

Remove this material from your folder, and staple each set of pages referring to the same job together. As you work on your summary, store your three sets of stapled answers plus the summary document in this folder. If you are interrupted in your work or want to write the summary over several work sessions, keep all of your work in this one manila folder in the pocket of your ring binder. Once you are done, you can place your tabbed answers for this chapter in their proper place, and add the summary as the last part of this chapter's writing.

Your learning style

To start describing your style(s) of learning, review your short entries in the 'tasks' question of the workbook. Quickly review all of your tasks for each of the three jobs. Return to the tasks and start looking for patterns that are similar over your work life.

You may notice common features to some of your tasks from different jobs. Where the tasks were similar, did you learn them the same way? If your answer is 'Yes', or even 'Yes, to some extent', can you see any pattern? If the tasks were very different but you notice that you learned them using similar means, does that similarity suggest that you have a certain 'learning style?' What would that be? Think of a word or phrase to describe it. Review the words you wrote to describe how you partially or completely learned the tasks. Write your own sentences in the present tense, and use active rather than passive words. Here is an example of a sentence you can write describing your observation.

For ___ kinds of tasks, I learn best by doing A, B, and C.

If you learned the same task one way in one job, and another way in a second job, this suggests that you have more than one style of learning. Most people do. Identify as many styles of learning by noting both the general and fine aspects of tasks where you employed these different styles. Continue this process until all of the tasks and your learning methods are accounted for.

Your own style

For many of us, our learning style doesn't fit any standard description. Is there anything in the Gardner list of eight intelligences that rings a bell for you? Remember, even though there are eight, people often combine these intelligences. There may even be intelligences or styles of learning not described in that list. If you consistently come up with ways of resolving problems that other people don't use, there is nothing wrong with naming 'your styles'. In naming them, try to use words that can be understood by others who would be trainers, teachers or educators for you. Use illustrations, music, art, stories and other creative means when simple words don't capture the essence of how you learn. Use any means that 'work' to help you communicate clearly with another person.

Using clear language to communicate about learning to employers

Before moving on to describe your style of working, is there anything you can say about your overall style of learning? Is there anything common to all the methods of learning you have described that allows you to say of yourself: 'I am a ____kind of learner?' You may be tempted to be critical or judgmental about your learning style. Avoid terms like 'lazy, stubborn, frustrated', or similar words. Use adjectives that are neutral or positive such as you would use in describing a building as 'tall' or a cornfield as 'flat'.

For those things you learn or partially learn, such descriptions are accurate reflections of how you learn, descriptions you can easily use when presenting yourself to others. They should describe 'how' you learn, so that people helping you can understand what you do to learn things best. To benefit from opportunities in your present or future jobs, it is important that you become a good self-advocate. Thus, you could describe your learning style to others like the examples below.

I learn best when I go step by step through a new process.

or

I learn best by not having to first hear (read, view) descriptions of how to do the whole job. I find that when I master each phase, I really appreciate the entire process much better and always perform my best.

Notice two things about these statements. First, they are 'I' statements, but they are not statements which indicate what your learning needs are. Whenever you sell yourself and your skills to a prospective employers you can use 'I' statements that don't refer to your needs. Discussion of your needs comes much later in the hiring process. When you present yourself as a person who knows what you learn well, and how you learn, employers and supervisors can imagine placing you in the position which best meets their needs.

The second thing to notice about the statements is that they are positive and truthful. They demonstrate insight and maturity. Many adults go through their lives without clearly understanding how they learn because learning has 'come naturally' to them. An employer may be inclined to think more of you for showing this extra insight, because it means you have deliberately taken the time to understand yourself. Learning some things doesn't come naturally to us. It probably never has. Your gaining an understanding about how you actually learn and how you really perform certain tasks is part of the purpose of this book.

Your working style

In describing how you work, follow the same process you used above summarizing your learning style.

It is common for some jobs to be difficult to perform. They may involve complex steps not easy to reduce to a routine, or which require completion only once in the job. Other tasks lend themselves to developing a routine, which you can perform on 'auto-pilot', or without much thought.

For similar tasks where you use the same style of work, describe the task in general terms, and describe how you do the task using a neutral or positive adjective. Examples of such adjectives are 'quickly', 'with great care', 'using past practice'.

The sentence below is an example.

When I do ____kind of work, I work (neutral/positive adjective).

Consider the next cluster of tasks where you used a different style of working. Using what is common with those tasks, write your next sentence like the one above. Continue this same process until you describe all of your tasks and work routines.

Sometimes it takes people a long time to develop a comfortable work style. At the end of your entries, try to find words that describe your overall work style, one which applies to the present. As with your description of yourself as a learner, do not use critical, negative or derogatory terms. Use neutral ones.

To describe how you see yourself as a worker, use the sentence below as a model.

I think of myself as a ____, ____, and ____ kind of worker.

It is now time for you to look at the other side of your learning and performance equation: your shortcomings. Review your responses to questions in Chapter 1 relating to your training and learning on the job. Is there a connection between your answers to those questions and particular tasks you had trouble learning?

Since you have already described in detail how you learned tasks, turn to the tasks you did *not* learn or perform well. Was there something your trainers or supervisors could have known about your learning needs to help you learn those tasks? Equally as important, are there things you now know about any learning disabilities you might have that can explain the problems you had or may still be experiencing? Ask yourself the same questions about the tasks you were unable to perform.

For adults, moving past some learning disabilities and performance limitations may be difficult or impossible. The question to ask of yourself is whether any challenges you are aware of are so much a problem that you cannot 'work around' them. There is nothing wrong with that. If you were to lose a limb, and having that limb is critical to your performance of an essential task at work, now would be the time to think of assistive technology or other reasonable accommodations that would preserve the job for you. Accommodations you ask for might not be reasonable in one employment setting but may be reasonable in others. Before you come to any conclusions about yourself, and about what you can and cannot learn and do, you have half of your employment biography still to write. There are more discoveries ahead.

4. Interests, Skills and Talents

It is now time to create your first master list. Your first master list refers to all of your interests, skills and talents, not just those related to your three jobs or the rest of your work. Your first list describes your passions and areas of specialized knowledge. In this first master list, you describe your personal assets. *Whether you are writing an abbreviated employment biography or a more complete history, you must write this first master list.*

If you are writing a complete employment history using a word processor, open a new document and title it 'Master List – Interests, Skills and Talents'. Copy entries on that list from the blank sheet at the beginning of Part 3, Section 4 with the same title.

Take a blank page of paper or open a new word processor document. Title it 'Master List – Interests, Skills and Talents'. Refer back to Chapter 5 in the first part of the book for definitions of these three terms. Start to list your assets in whatever order you wish.

Write your list without considering whether the items relate to your jobs. Include everything; even your 'secrets'. Be kind to yourself. Do not compare yourself with anyone else or exclude things that other people consider unusual, strange or weird. Do not think that because you are less skillful than another person that your skill does not count. List your talents whether you use them or not. Leave enough space between your entries to identify parents, relatives, teachers, trainers, and mentors who encouraged you with your interest, skill or talent. If you developed interests as a youth or as an adult that you used in work, circle them or identify them with a special symbol. From this point forward, use your master list in reviewing your three jobs.

Open your ring binder and find your page in the first chapter where you describe 'All My Jobs'. Review the list. Successful workers use their talents, skills or interests in their work. Before you focus on the three jobs representative of your early, middle and late work periods, use the list to identify other jobs where you used other interests, skills and talents you forgot to enter on your master list. Add those items to your master list now.

Your workbook responses describing your job tasks are found in Question 13. Other questions from the first section of the workbook also relate to the conditions of your jobs, including the environment, social expectations, and other features.

Open your ring binder. Locate the tabbed set of written sentences and paragraphs for your first job. Leave them in the binder, but open the binder so that you can refer to them. In this workbook turn back to Question 13, and leave your workbook open at this question.

Take a manila folder and title it: 'Interests, Skills and Talents'. Temporarily store material you write for this chapter in this folder until your writing for all three jobs is complete. At the end of each work session, until you are done, remember to store the folder in the pocket of your ring binder.

If you are writing an abbreviated employment history, you can decide how much detail you wish to include in writing about how you have used your assets in each job. You can start to write this information down on the 'short list' pages for each of your jobs.

Take a new page or open up a new document in your word processor. On the upper right hand corner, write 'First Job'. Title the page, 'Interests, Skills and Talents'. Attach the same color tab as your other first job writings. Consult your written material to the answers you wrote for Question 13. Consult your first period job description. If you review your master list, you have all the material you need to write about the assets you brought to each task of that job. Write about how you developed them and acquired new ones for that job. Complete your writing for one job before you turn to the next one.

Follow the same process for your middle-period and late-period jobs. For each, make a new page or open a new word processor page for these jobs. Title them appropriately, and apply the proper colored tab identifying which of your three jobs they belong to. Complete your written work in the same way as you did for your first job.

The Illustration below (4.1) shows you what materials should be on your desktop to work on one of your jobs.

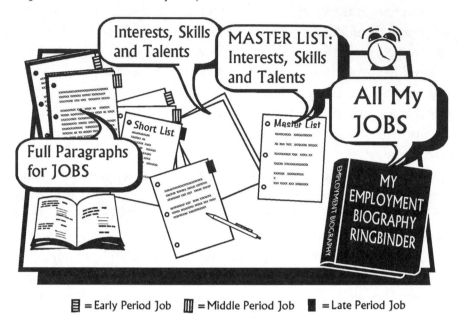

Illustration 4.1

Going clockwise from the upper left hand corner are the following items. Gathered together at the upper left hand corner are all the pages you have written to describe each of your jobs in detail. To the right are your short lists. They are described below. As you review the other data about each job, add the interest, skills or talents that occur to you as you read. To the right of blank pages on which you will make written entries is your master list for this section. In the illustration, the writer is in the midst of composing a page of full paragraphs for the late period job from the 'short list' words and phrases.

Writing tips

To help you get started, you might prefer to make an abbreviated list of all your assets that you brought or developed in the job. Call this your 'short list'. You can then write your sentences and paragraphs using the list as an outline.

On your pages for each of the jobs, identify each task and write about the personal assets you brought, developed, or used to perform it. Use your master list as a guide, and add any others you remember that related to the job. Add these newly remembered assets to your master list. If other people recognized your assets, describe how their knowledge of your strengths affected your work. If one or more of your tasks used none of your assets, go on to the next task.

One possible way of describing your assets would be to review the eight multiple intelligence categories found in Chapter 3 as a way of further refining your discussion. Include any other insights gained from assessing your styles of learning and work in Part 3 Section 3 of the workbook. In your writing, try to draw upon any nuances and interconnections between your interests, skills and talents. Be creative in your observations, but also be precise and accurate. You may be returning to your writing in the future, and it is best to write so as not to cause you a lot of work later figuring out what you mean.

An example

Here are sample paragraphs written by a person in his mid-thirties. The author writes about his middle-period job. Remember, some people have an important first period of work even before they finish college, and that is the case here.

This job was the first and most important job I held right after college. I had pursued my interest in habitat recovery throughout the last two years of high school by working on summer projects in two raptor protection areas in the Olympia National Forest. In my junior and senior years of college I also did paid summer work assisting in the Condor breeding project in California. Because of my contacts, I went through a quick interview with the State Parks and Wildlife Department, and was hired as a Naturalist II. My supervisor was the man I had worked with in the Condor project. My knowledge about raptors, and my experience in habitat recovery got me into a project where the state Department of Agriculture was working with loggers and sheep and cattle ranchers to prevent the loss of nesting habitat for two species of threatened list owls and one threatened list hawk.

I was responsible for drawing together all the easy-to-read literature. Because I was familiar with most of it, I knew which materials were out of date or wrong, and substituted new articles and a couple of my quickie papers I wrote during the Olympic National Forest summers. I also designed and conducted education sessions with individual farmers, ranchers and loggers. I had learned how to do the individual consultations from accompanying my supervisor to similar sessions during my Washington State summers jobs, and from coaching high school students with their FFA [Future Farmers of America] projects for the state fair. I also got help from a department trainer who gave me a lot of teaching tips.

I didn't deal with our conferences because organizing them was too much, and I really liked working one-on-one with different kinds of people. While our project had certain objectives to meet, we were seen as non-threatening because of our individual approach to each person we worked with. On a couple of occasions, the dairy ranchers invited our whole team to an annual convention. I was uncomfortable in the large meeting, but I knew so many of the people there that it seemed to make things better. In the second conference, I even did a little impromptu workshop for some land-use planners whose properties were beginning threaten the farms next to Hill City. It was all question and answer stuff, but I think that is the best way to learn.

5. My Work and Asperger Syndrome

- *If you intend to use just the workbook pages to assess the role of AS on your work, you lose an opportunity for some serious reflection. Consider doing all of the work outlined in these instructions. Helping you understand the connection between your particular flavor of AS and the world of work is the central purpose of this book.*

In this chapter you will draw on your understanding of how Asperger Syndrome has made you a unique person and in what respects AS has influenced your work life.

Refer to the list of *Asperger Syndrome Characteristics* in Appendix I. The purpose of completing this section of the workbook is to identify just those characteristics applicable to your experience in three jobs. It may be tempting for you to become rather morose when you read the full list. This is understandable. Sometimes when we view ourselves through the lenses of others – in this case, 'experts' in the medical field – we tend to think of ourselves in the role of 'victim', or at least 'patient'. In completing this workbook section, you are neither. You are a worker.

To write this chapter, I ask you to keep your focus on your three jobs and be an honest reporter about yourself. Use the list as a reference when thinking about your own flavor of AS and work. It is not a Bible. I don't expect you to beat yourself up in the process of discovery about yourself. Others have been very good at doing that to you. There is no need for you to join that crowd. Self-understanding is the first step – and the most important step – to self-determination. We will explore that topic later in this workbook in the last section on diagnosis, disclosure and self-advocacy.

Review before writing

To start your work in this chapter, open the book to Appendix I. Spend some time reading the list. Then turn to your 'short answers' in the workbook, Sections 1 through 4. Review them quickly.

If you are using a word processor to write your employment biography, create three blank documents of two pages each. Title your documents 'My Work and Asperger Syndrome', and designate each set of two pages 'early', 'middle' and 'late' for your three jobs. When you have completed your written entries, print the pages and tab each set with the color chosen for its period.

Your short lists

If you use the workbook for this exercise, note that the first six pages of Section 5 of the workbook are blank. Each set of two pages refers to one job. On these pages, you will compose a 'short list' of the AS manifestations you expressed at the job. Use the terms and phrases from Appendix I. Do not make up your own terms to describe your AS manifestations. In making your list for each job, avoid the 'kitchen sink' approach of applying all of your AS behaviors to the job. Do not force any connections. Just as your behaviors are your own, so the connections are your own. Do not ask anyone to assist you with this work. *Your* answers are the only ones that matter.

Once your short list for each job is complete, you can start to write sentences and paragraphs about how those AS characteristics impacted on your work. To focus on how your learning and work styles reflect your AS, review your answers to Question 13. To concentrate on your communication and social skills, review your answers in the Social Skills section, at Question 74.

On the page sets, write your entries according to the four categories of Asperger characteristics found on the *Asperger Syndrome Characteristics* list. The categories are:

- Physical manifestations
- Work characteristics
- Cognitive characteristics
- Social characteristics.

Until you are completely done writing this chapter, keep all of this loose material in your Chapter 5 manila folder. Between work sessions, place the folder in the ring binder pocket for safekeeping.

Your summaries

Take out three more blank pages if you are writing or typing. If you are using a word processor, instead of opening new documents, treat these 'additional pages' as continuations of your three documents for this chapter. On each of these new pages, write the title, 'Summary: My Work and Asperger Syndrome', and add information from the instructions found below. Illustration 5.1 shows you how this material should look spread out on your worktop.

Once you have reviewed your tasks for the job and listed which AS characteristics came into play for those tasks, turn to the second set of pages if you are writing or typing, or continue your written work in the word processor document. With all three short lists in front of you, notice whether characteristics you and others felt were in the way of your work appear across all of the tasks, or just some of them. The writing you do in the form of sentences and paragraphs should completely cover each abbreviated entry you made on your lists. Disturbing AS manifestations may have appeared while you learned your tasks or performed them. If they did, indicate how they affected your stress level as you struggled with the task and with getting them under control.

= Early Period Job   = Middle Period Job   = Late Period Job

Illustration 5.1

If you suppressed some AS characteristics at work that could have made learning or performing the task(s) easier, write about it. In your reflection, include your thoughts about how distracting those manifestations might have been to your co-workers if you had let them occur. Is there any way you could have substituted less distracting behaviors or attitudes? What alternative behaviors do you think may have been more acceptable to others?

At a later point in your employment biography, you can decide whether some high-stress tasks are so taxing to you that you'd rather avoid them now or in the future. On the other hand, if you still want to continue doing that kind of work, you could decide to either make workplace accommodations to reduce your stress, or change your behavioral reactions to the stress.

If your work history involves completely different kinds of work, and your job choice in each work period reflects those differences, it is likely that some AS manifestations were of more concern at one time than at others. If your jobs tend to be related or are quite similar, such variation may not be so noticeable. For some jobs, you might recall certain behaviors occurring at one period during the time span of the whole job but were of less concern at other times.

Even with a particular task, the same may be true at the beginning, middle, or completion of that task. How your AS manifestations shifted or changed may indicate particular times of challenge or periods of good performance in your job. These are important differences to note as you write your sentences and paragraphs describing how AS affects your work.

As with your previous chapters, write complete sentences and organize each paragraph around a single topic or cluster of related topics.

Some tips and an example

To start your paragraph writing, start with the category 'Physical Manifestations'. Review the questions and your workbook responses relating to the conditions and environment of the job.

Physical conditions such as working in a noisy, fast paced setting may increase sensitivity to noise or work pace both at work and elsewhere. The same conditions could also contribute to a need to 'wind down', recover, or to be completely inactive following a strenuous day at work.

The conditions need not be physical. For example, if your pay was inadequate or if you had poor or no health benefits, these matters could very well cause an increase in sleep disturbance, depression, stim behavior and anxiety.

Expand on any connections you make between the work situation and your own AS. Where an AS characteristic contributed to job success, describe how it did so. For example, perseverance and attention to detail are valued attributes in programming, translating, editing, research and archival work, jobs requiring sensory attention such as media and the arts, music performance, mathematics, advocacy and education. Scrupulous honesty is important to accounting, financial management, statistical research, actuarial, risk management and insurance work, and product evaluation. Expert knowledge about obscure or little known subjects is important in legal research, advocacy work, most academic work and in troubleshooting and systems design.

The paragraphs below illustrate the role played by several AS manifestations in a particular job. Here, the writer uses the category 'Cognitive Characteristics'.

Although I was on a 'team' of quality control engineers, we each worked independently and our ratings were compared by the safety and production supervisors. I was in charge of the welding work on all hydraulic, pneumatic, acids and corrosive solution supply, vent and drain lines for one whole side of the fab plant. Parallel systems served the other side. Many skilled trades people were constantly involved in modification and new work, and the plant operated with three work shifts. I worked with a high level of focus following work on each line from storage, pump, interface to the plant building through the maze of services on the intermediate level to the equipment and back on recycle, recovery, and disposal.

We all wore special uniforms, and everyone was instructed not to talk to us or distract us during our 'runs'. I am uncomfortable wearing uniforms, but this was an exception. Since I am easily distracted, the uniform saved me from a lot of hassles with other people. The other inspectors felt constrained by the no-talking rule, but I was in heaven. We all had to follow the same inspection protocols to the letter with no variation, and that was perfect for me. Each of us wrote an 'ideal' set of protocols, and all three batches were submitted to the division manager, who then selected from our rules to come up with a uniform routine. That way it was hard for us to question the rules since we wrote them. I liked that process rather than being handed a set written by someone who doesn't do the work and who doesn't come up against new challenges every day.

I am a visual learner, and being able to connect instructions with real objects is easy. I like to handle and manipulate things to test them out and literally get a feel of what is going on. I was relieved to work with others who were better at writing out the first to last steps of a procedure. When I interviewed for the position, the supervisor asked me about how I set priorities and establish sequences for doing the work. I told her this was a problem for me, but I was eager to work in a setup that allowed my shortcomings to be compensated by the contributions of others. Some of my experience was of equal value to the other inspectors, so I felt this was a good trade-off. She agreed.

I work best when there is a known way to accomplish things. She let me know that if I thought of a different or better way of doing something that rather than convince the other inspectors, I could talk directly with her. She always got back to me about these suggestions. She knew I couldn't handle public compliments, so she was careful about how she introduced a change I proposed. I was very grateful for the letters of commendation she wrote for my personnel file.

When you are done writing your paragraphs about one job, place your papers in the folder, and turn to the next job. When your work for all three is complete, let your writing sit, unread, for at least a day.

Conclusions

Your last 'assignment' for this section is voluntary, but very worthwhile. Take out a new page or open a new word processor document and title it, 'My Conclusions – My Work and Asperger Syndrome'. I encourage you to revisit your writing for all three jobs and compose some final comments that reflect changes and personal development you observe as you matured. For the first part of your summary, I propose that you ignore all of the limitations which your AS has imposed on your work. It is unlikely that as you mature that everything has gotten worse, although this does happen to some people. Most of us do learn from our 'mistakes'. Even though deliberate change may be hard for many of us, change nevertheless occurs on its own, often as a function of our aging and exposure to more of life. Like a sharp mountain rock loosed during an avalanche and ending up in a swift running mountain stream, as we tumble through life our sharp edges get knocked off. Most of us get less rattled by the same events as we age. Though with age comes greater vulnerability and loss of resilience, we often learn how to protect ourselves from harm.

In a word, with age comes wisdom.

For your first paragraph, consider the following idea. Look for manifestations that have become more manageable over the total time spread of your three jobs. Describe any changes for the better. Don't magnify them beyond their true impact, but don't ignore even the small ones especially if you feel you can do more to hasten greater change.

The purpose of your writing is not to reinforce your ideas of what you can't do. By this point in your life, and through your chapters in your work biography, you already know about your limitations. As you consider what is possible to change, bear in mind that you are not defined by your limitations. For the most part, other people know you for what you *can* do, not what you can't do or haven't done.

It is good to be honest about things that give you trouble. You may wish to make brief mention of those things in your summary. By now you are the expert on them. One difference between us and neurotypical persons with the same limitations is that for many of them, their shortcomings may not bother them all that much. We tend to ruminate about ours. We do something more. We talk about them a lot. Everyone goes through life stubbing his or her toes. Healthy people don't go through life telling others they are toe-stubbers. What benefit is derived from that?

We may decide that personal work on this trait is important to us in our present job. It may be even more important in our future work.

So often we carry a mental image of ourselves that is at odds with our obvious strengths. Many of us adopt a survivor-mentality. We are so used to stumbling and being bruised that we often can't see our own healing and growth. Think of your role in writing your employment story as an explorer. Most explorers take risks to learn new things not only for themselves, but also for others. Work involves yourself and others. Keep this fact in mind as you write your conclusions.

6. Personal Tools and Strategies

- *Even if you are writing an abbreviated employment biography, follow the instructions below. You must complete this work for the biography to be a guide for your future.*

For this section of the workbook, you create your second master list. In the list you can describe how you handle difficult situations. When you finish this section of the workbook, you will see the connections between your survival techniques and your work life accomplishments.

Your master list

Take a manila folder, and on the front write: 'Personal Tools and Strategies.' Place all of your loose sheets within the folder and store the folder in the inside pocket of your ring binder until your written work for this chapter is complete.

The first three pages of this section in the workbook are titled: 'Master List – Tools and Strategies'. Record your entries there. If you need more paper, use additional paper and give the sheets the same title. If you are composing your employment biography on a computer, match what is done in the workbook. Open a new document and title it: 'Master List – Tools and Strategies'.

It may be difficult for you to start making entries in your master list. Here is a suggestion that may help.

Try an exercise. To do this exercise, find a place where you can talk out loud to yourself without appearing ridiculous to other people. Start by talking out loud as if you were telling a story to another person. Recall a situation from your early childhood where you remember being in trouble and managed to escape in good shape. Try to remember:

- What happened

- Who was there

- Where it happened

- When, in time, it happened

- What you did to get through the event.

Do not try to recall 'why' you did what you did. It happened. Simple as that. You did something that worked. 'Why' is your logical adult talking. Remember, when the incident occurred, you were not thinking with adult logic. You had your own logic, and that was good enough. Even if you asked for help and got it, you did the asking. Asking for help is a strategy. The tools you have in your tool kit are much like this. People use them to get out of trouble, to meet challenges and overcome obstacles. For this first event, then, describe it, and describe your 'fix'.

Turn to your master list. Write: 'Asking for Help'.

Continue telling yourself these stories and from each story describe the strategy or tool you used. Recall as many as you can. From later work in this chapter, you will be adding many more tools to your master list. You will be consulting it as you identify the tools and strategies you used for survival in each of your three jobs.

A list for each job

The next three pages in this section of the workbook are blank except for their title and designation of your job. As you progress through each job, record the tools you used for each task identified in Question 13 for your three jobs. Your resource materials for writing this chapter of your employment biography include your already-completed written work for each job. As with your work elsewhere in this workbook, use the pages of the workbook and extra sheets of paper titled and tabbed for each job. If you are use a word processor, open three documents and copy the appearance of the workbook pages. As you print your work, color tab the first page of each and keep the other sheets for that job together with its first page.

You now have five sections' worth of workbook responses completed for each job. As with the last section of the workbook you completed, use your short workbook responses as a quick reference. If there isn't enough detail in your workbook responses, consult your tabbed, written material for that job. You now have complete information on the job itself, your understanding of the social skills required to perform it, your learning and work styles, your interests, skills and talents, and how your AS manifested itself in each job. All of this information relates to how you used your survival tools when faced with challenges at work.

Once you review your responses to questions in each of the previous sections of the workbook, you may discover new survival tools you fashioned for the moment or for the whole job. Before you write about them, name them and add them to your master list of personal tools and strategies. As you progress through the chapters, your master list will grow.

Illustration 6.1 shows you the materials you should have on your worktop at this point. The drawing represents the way in which you add items to your master list as you recall them from each job, and, finally, how you assess the overall current value of these personal tools and strategies.

Take your first page for the first job, and make a short list of your survival tools by turning to Question 13 in the first section of the workbook. There, you outlined information about the actual tasks of your job. For each task learned or partially learned, what tricks or shortcuts did you use to resolve difficulties you encountered? Confine your answers to the severe problems you faced, rather than just routine ones. Go through each task and identify the tools you used.

Once you complete your review of a job's specific tasks, look at your other workbook answers in Section 1 concerning the environment or general conditions of that job. Write about how you overcame obstacles, managed your sensitivities, and used some of your AS characteristics to your advantage in surviving on the job. Describe the methods you used to address environmental challenges and social demands. For example, how did you deal with bad work hours, the

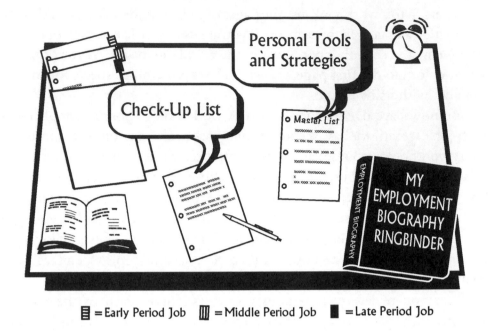

Illustration 6.1

need to take time off, vacations, medical appointments, and sensory assaults (high noise levels, troublesome lighting, odors)? How did you handle expectations to attend employer-provided social or recreational events, requests by others that you join them in social events at and away from work, and bad company management practices? While some of these challenges are subtle, if you were aware of them that means that you made a response to them. Remember the most bothersome problems you faced, and how you dealt with them. If you avoided or ignored a problem, avoidance or ignoring is also a response. It is a tool, and depending upon how you handled the situation, it could either have been a good or a bad one.

Start a new paragraph. Look at your workbook responses for Section 2. What did you substitute for weak or absent social skills to make those skills seem less important to your fellow workers and supervisors? Describe your work-arounds, and how you successfully bypassed social challenges so as not to offend or affect others negatively. If you met a difficult social challenge successfully, describe what you did to overcome it. That is a survival tool.

To review the role of your learning and work style in Section 3 of the workbook, return to the first section and Question 13 to refresh your memory about how you learned and performed each task. If you felt better because of having done or said something that reduced your discomfort as you *learned* a particular kind of task and at the same time built a positive reputation for yourself, write about that. Describe how the way you *worked* had a similar positive effect. If it was an entirely new way of working, or if you took special measures to perform a very difficult task, make a note of these occurrences. These are additional survival strategies.

In reviewing your written material for Section 4 of the workbook, did any of your interests, skills and talents contribute to your feeling of success on the job? Were there any that were so prominent as to be called a survival tool? If so, name it, and add it to your master list.

Which of your AS characteristics made tasks easier for you? Which manifestations set you ahead of your fellow workers? Describe them, and describe how you handled your advanced knowledge or techniques. Handling success is a skill. If you handled your own success well, it is a survival tool. If you feel positive about your success, others will be encouraged to feel the same way about theirs, especially if you acknowledge their success openly. If you handled your success and that of others well, this fact can make the difference between retention and promotion on the job, and remaining where you are or being let go when business takes a downturn.

At each point you encounter a tip, trick, or survival strategy, make sure you note it for the job and add it to your master list.

Your master list is your big toolbox. It contains all of your survival tools. If you are considering major changes at your present job or a completely different kind of job in the future, your master list is an inventory of the skills you developed to face and conquer problems in the past and the present. If you run into unexpected difficulties in your current that job, or know that certain difficulties come 'built into' the job, you can hold these tools up and scrutinize the fit between your tool and the problem. You may have performed this process many times in the past. See if it fits a new job with tasks similar or identical to those of a past job. Keep your master list in mind. It will prepare you for problems in advance. It may help you avoid panic searches for a fix during very stressful times.

A text example, a list, and some comments

Below is an example of paragraphs describing one person's techniques for meeting several related task challenges in a middle-period job. At the end of the text is a list of survival tools the writer used on the job.

As the assistant produce manager, I often did the back-floor work along with the other produce clerks. When I first started, I was really distracted by the view of the retail floor from the large picture window in front of the trimming sinks. I was always being startled by the sounds of the service doors and truck ramp doors slamming. My balance isn't very good either, and the wet floors made me feel I was walking on slick ice. Our store was undergoing a remodel, and I made several suggestions for changes where I didn't have to reveal my hypersensitivity and balance issues to anyone. They were accepted because they improved overall safety and production rates. I reduced door slamming and overall shipping and receiving noise levels by proposing laser door switches and hydraulic closers for the service doors. They built a firewall between storage and processing, and the shipping/receiving areas. Before that was even started, the insurance guy came around, I mentioned the noise, and he measured the sound levels in our area. Fortunately, they were higher than that allowed for no hearing protection, so we were all issued earplugs. That helped a lot. My manager mentioned this in our next storewide safety meeting. Not only did it reduce stress, but it also exposed the store to fewer hearing-loss claims.

The smooth concrete floor was always wet, and any trimmings from the produce guaranteed a slip and fall. Because I wasn't the only one who felt unsafe on it, I talked with the section manager and he got hard rubber anti-skid perforated floor mats. I felt uncomfortable 'working in a fish bowl,' so I mentioned it to my manager and he agreed it was a problem, and that none of the clerks liked it either. We both agreed that the view in by customers was not as important as the one a customer wants in the meat and deli sections. I suggested the store could block the window and put rack shelving and display graphics in the area outside. The store manager liked the idea, since we were in the midst of a store remodel. I arranged to have additional bacterial suppression lighting placed directly over the sinks, something that needed to happen anyway because the light was so bad even with the window, and, in three days this was all done. By relating to the work discomfort of others, I avoided having to tell anyone that visual distraction is a major problem for me. The resolution was win-win all around.

List of survival tools used on the job

- Depersonalizing my hypersensitivity to noise, visual distractions and balance problems by showing how others are similarly affected by the same dangerous conditions.

- Making positive suggestions for change at the right time to the right person.

- Accepting commendation well for an improvement beneficial to all workers and to the employer.

- Getting others to appreciate a problem by involving them in its solution.

- Taking advantage of chaos (remodeling) to correct an old problem and making positive improvements for the business with minimum disruption to ongoing work.

Comment

Any one of these strategies is more than a mere survival tool. Each one is an accomplishment that the writer can mention when asked about his value to the workplace and his ability to work under trying conditions. Each one is directly related to the worker's personal survival on the job. Any prospective employer can see the value to his survival behavior as a future employee. Many employers use a technique of interviewing known as 'behavioral interviewing'. They want to hear stories from applicants that relate to past challenges in their work and how they resolved them. The example above is such a story. In each use of a survival tool, the writer in this example included others as justification for his own personal action. This deflected attention from what were clearly personal issues to include others in a larger picture. Whether or not there is a management job in the future for the writer, it is clear that his thinking involved the welfare of others as a part of his total view of the workplace. This is what the writer has in mind when he describes his experiences as 'win-win' situations. Accommodations do not have to be costly to be of mutual benefit to an employer and a disabled employee. In this case, the writer didn't have to share the fact of his AS issues with his employer to get what he needed – and more – out of the situation.

Time for a tune up?

By completing your paragraphs and working through your jobs chronologically, you may notice a difference in how some of your survival skills work over time. Before returning your pages to the ring binder, read them in one sitting. If your use of any survival tool has changed, you can judge how well an early-acquired strategy works now. It may be time for a tool box checkup and inspection.

The last two pages of the workbook for this section are titled 'Tool Maintenance and Check-up List'. If you are using a word processor to compose your employment biography, create a new document with same heading as this section and title it the same way as the pages in the workbook. After you finish your work with this list, you are done with the written work for this section. Place your printed pages behind the divider in the ring binder with this section's title already written on it.

Write about any changes you observe in your use of certain survival strategies over your entire work life. Consider the following points while writing this material:

- Identify job-related strategies that no longer work for you. Explain to yourself why they don't work any more.

- Look at your master list. Name tools unrelated to employment that do not work for you now in other parts of your adult life. Determine whether you want to keep them or discard them.

Identify work and personal AS-related challenges you would like to overcome or bypass in order to get hired, keep a job, and be promoted in the job. For the moment, treat this as a mental exercise. Start with something simple. The idea is not to come up with solutions. For now, just list your issues. When you finish writing this list, attach three tabs to it. Doing this will make it easy for you to find the list in your ring binder. After you finish writing with your complete employment autobiography, schedule a return to this page.

A tip for those who want to experiment with a solution

Up to now, thinking of a 'solution' should only be a mental exercise. You haven't yet considered all of the factors involved in actually trying out a solution. Once you get used to the idea of experimenting with a 'fix' in your head, you can continue this 'thought experiment' to a second stage.

You might be tempted at this time to try something out for real, not just in your head. There are two intermediate steps you should take before you actually go for a real solution.

- First, experiment with a solution by talking out loud to yourself. Go ahead and try it. Remember my warnings about doing this in a safe place.

- Second, find a safe person and talk about your solution. Do not try it out 'on the job'. You will find this work difficult if not impossible to successfully do by yourself. Not being able to do this by yourself has to do with the neurobiological, cognitive features of being an autistic person. Seek out a person who offers you the opportunity to do a 'dry run'. Finding such a person provides you with a reality check. In the hands of a skilled professional, a person who understands Asperger Syndrome and is experienced in cognitive behavioral therapy, you can 'depersonalize' your proposed solution, and consider it as though it is an object of study. Once you have taken the solution apart step by step, you can create scripts and 'what if's' to your heart's content. Knowing when and how to use the solution is the hardest work of being an autistic worker.

- When you feel you are ready, work with the professional to test your solution on something very benign, something not related to work. Whatever you do, don't look on a result less than perfect as a failure. Once you see progress and believe you can do it, you are on your way to creating a good new tool.

The survival tools and strategies developed throughout your lifetime which work well for you now are similar to those things you would need if you were marooned on a desert island. The difference between these tools and the other things you bring to that island is that no one can take these tools away from you. You can use them on the island and in everyday life in society.

Before you consider going for a solution on the job, complete the work in the last two sections of this workbook.

7. Diagnosis, Disclosure and Self-advocacy

- *If you are writing an abbreviated employment biography, the questions in Section 7 of the workbook provide your instructions. If you wish to expand on your answers, you can add additional pages with this section title to your ring binder.*

Diagnosis and disclosure issues are those that 'hit closest to home'. If you are an autistic person, you 'know' that because you have self-diagnosed or received your diagnosis from a professional. You will wrestle with the issue of disclosure for the rest of your life. In the language of advocacy, your self-determination (self-discovery) is the first step to becoming a good self-advocate. You completed part of that process by writing about the impact of your AS in your work life. Knowledge you gained by answering the workbook questions through Question 74 prepared you for this role.

Before starting your written work for workbook Questions 75 through 101, you may wish to re-read the first chapter of the book. As you consider disclosure issues at work, you need not confine your thinking to the three jobs you chose. If you have held more than one job since your diagnosis, feel free to discuss disclosure issues that came up in all of them.

If you use a computer or word processor to compose your work history, open a new document and title it 'Diagnosis, Disclosure and Self-Advocacy'. Read through all questions before you begin to write your sentences and paragraphs. If there are some questions that don't apply to your experience, mark them with an 'NA' so that when you write your sentences and paragraphs, you will know that you considered it. Illustration 7.1 is a depiction of your worktop.

As you write about your experience, the order in which you answer the questions is entirely up to you. If you have not disclosed your AS at work, this is your chance to thoroughly explore the costs and gains of doing so. There are no right or wrong answers relating to your decision(s). Don't decide ahead of time what the outcome of your thinking will be and then censor your thoughts to fit that outcome. Consider everything, including the effect of your decision on persons who are not at work. Your thoughts about disclosure at work may assist you in disclosing your AS in non-employment situations.

Illustration 7.1

The workbook has two blank pages titled 'Reflections on my Disclosure Experiences'. Use these pages to record any differences between employment situations where accommodations have differed. If you disclosed your AS to your employer or co-workers at more than one job, you may have done it differently and encountered different reactions in each instance. Accommodations arranged for you may have been different. You might have had some employment experiences where you were more upfront about your AS. They may have been followed by work situations where being as open about your AS wasn't (or isn't) a good idea. If this has been your experience, write about these different experiences in a final summary set of paragraphs.

Be careful about putting your thoughts about disclosure into action. At the close of Chapter 2 in the first part of this book are some factors that should figure into your action plan. Read them.

8. My Wish List

These instructions refer to the last section of the workbook. The first three pages of the last section of the workbook contain a list of questions to start you thinking about your future as a worker. They are only a start. Whether you write an abbreviated employment biography or a lengthy version, if you answer some or all of them, you will probably think of many more.

When you write your own wish list, you can identify the steps you need to take charge of planning for your future. There are two additional blank pages following the checklist on which you can jot down your first thoughts. If you use a computer or word processor, start a new document entitled 'My Wish List – Notes to Myself'. Unlike many of your materials from earlier sections of the workbook, your wish list should remain open for future entries. Like your list of tools and survival strategies, your wish list is subject to change and modification throughout the rest of your work life. Illustration 8.1 below is a depiction of what you should have on your worktop to start this process.

Most of the list questions involve connecting up with others. They prompt you to act socially, but on terms that allow you to feel comfortable. But not too comfortable. The reason you may be seeking something different for yourself is that you aren't comfortable with certain things. If you were, there would be no sense to reading this book and writing your employment biography.

Things change. Much of what changes is not subject to our control. One purpose for seeking the assistance of others should be our knowledge that we have trouble with change and we always have. The purpose of this book is to put you more in charge of change than you have been in the past.

We also have trouble asking for help. In fact, most of us have such trouble with asking for help that we don't even know that we need it. We have become 'experts in denial'. I don't feel that denial is an expertise that should be indulged or cultivated. For those of us watching change leave us behind, denying that we must change in order to survive is dysfunctional. In addition to having trouble with change, we have major challenges in planning. You can't plan in a vacuum. Your plans must be made with reference to the future and must involve other people. Even if you plan to be self-employed, you will have customers, suppliers, and support persons needed to help you with your business.

Illustration 8.1

If you have answered questions in the workbook and written chapters for your employment history, you have already started to think of your future differently than before you began your work. What you wish to change, how much, at what rate, and in what order, is up to you.

PART 3

Workbook

SECTION I

THREE JOBS
ALL MY JOBS

THREE JOBS
ALL MY JOBS

First Job of Three – *Early Period*

1. My job title was _____

2. I learned about the job from *(Please circle. You can select more than one answer)*

    advertisement: TV, radio, printed announcement or public notice •
    job fair • family member or friend • employment counselor;
    vocational rehabilitation counselor • job placement agency (school
    placement service, temporary agency) • word of mouth • school or
    program official • other (be specific)

3. I was hired mainly due to my:

    informal education and training • formal education and training •
    previous experience in identical or related work • knowing someone
    inside • referral by a family member or friend • referral by a third
    party • appearance and presentation in the interview • other
    (describe)

4. I was:

    employed by others • self-employed • other (describe)

5. I worked mainly:

    outside • inside • in varied locations

6. My hours were _____

    full time • part time (How many hours?) • varied • other (describe)

7. The number of hours I worked were _____

    too many for me at the time • about right for me at the time • too
    few for me at the time

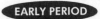

8. I was paid by _____ *(select one)*

> piecework • commission • salary plus commission • salary • hourly
> wage • barter or scrip • by the job (contract work) • not paid • other
> (describe)

9. I had _____ benefits coverage *(Benefits include unpaid leave,*
vacation, health, dental, retirement, employee discounts, etc.)

> full • some • little • no

10. There was _____ promotion and advancement
    opportunity.

> unlimited • some • little • no

11. I thought my pay was _____

> very good • good • adequate • bad • very bad

12. My employer was _____ accommodating when I needed
    time away from work, flexible work hours, leaves of absence,
    vacation and compensatory time.

> very • somewhat • rarely • never

*On the following pages for Question 13, there are spaces for you to describe each **major** task and responsibility of the job. If you had more tasks than allowed for in the pages in this section of the chapter, duplicate the last page as many times as you need. Add additional letters identifying each new task.*

*After you have identified and described your tasks, further describe the task by indicating how hard the task was to learn and how much of it you learned to do. Use the letters under those questions as shorthand answers. Leave the answering of the questions about how you learned the tasks and how you actually performed them until later. You will return to these two items and complete them when you work through Section 3 on **Learning and Work Styles**.*

13. Job Tasks and Responsibilities

TASK   Learning Difficulty

(A)_____   Hard (H)   Easy (E)

_____   Learned?

_____   Yes (Y)   Partially (P)   No (N)

_____

What I did to learn the task:

How I did the task:

13. Job Tasks and Responsibilities

TASK   Learning Difficulty

(B)_____   Hard (H)   Easy (E)

_____
_____   Learned?

_____   Yes (Y)   Partially (P)   No (N)

_____

What I did to learn the task:

How I did the task:

13. Job Tasks and Responsibilities

TASK

(C)_____

_____

_____

_____

_____

Learning Difficulty

Hard (H)   Easy (E)

Learned?

Yes (Y)   Partially (P)   No (N)

What I did to learn the task:

How I did the task:

13. Job Tasks and Responsibilities

TASK   Learning Difficulty

(D)_____   Hard (H)   Easy (E)

_____

_____   Learned?

_____   Yes (Y)   Partially (P)   No (N)

_____

What I did to learn the task:

How I did the task:

13. Job Tasks and Responsibilities

TASK

(E)_____

_____

_____

_____

_____

Learning Difficulty

Hard (H)   Easy (E)

Learned?

Yes (Y)   Partially (P)   No (N)

What I did to learn the task:

How I did the task:

13. Job Tasks and Responsibilities

TASK

(F)_____

_____

_____

_____

_____

Learning Difficulty

Hard (H)   Easy (E)

Learned?

Yes (Y)   Partially (P)   No (N)

What I did to learn the task:

How I did the task:

13. Job Tasks and Responsibilities

TASK   Learning Difficulty

(G)_____   Hard (H)   Easy (E)

_____

_____   Learned?

_____   Yes (Y)   Partially (P)   No (N)

_____

What I did to learn the task:

How I did the task:

13. Job Tasks and Responsibilities

TASK   Learning Difficulty

(H)_____   Hard (H)   Easy (E)

_____

_____   Learned?

_____   Yes (Y)   Partially (P)   No (N)

_____

What I did to learn the task:

How I did the task:

14. Once I was hired, my training consisted of _____
   (If appropriate, select more than one answer.)

   formal class training • job and training manuals • formal
   trainer/mentor • informal trainer/mentor • other (be specific)

15. I made _____ use of my **prior** skills, preparation, training
   and experience in the job?

   full • partial • little • no

16. *This question relates to your comfort level during three phases of your job, a
   beginning period, a middle period, and the period at the end of the time you held
   the job. For each of these periods, describe additional duties you were given for the
   job, and how prepared you were for the tasks when they were assigned. You may
   choose only two answers for each time. From the answers below, select the answers
   that best describe your feeling of readiness for those additional tasks.*

   (A) When I first got the job I felt _____ to take on
      additional tasks assigned to me.

      I had the skill • I had the training • I did not have the skill •
      I did not have the training

   (B) After I had gotten used to the job and was in a middle period,
      I felt _____ to take on additional
      tasks assigned to me.

      I had the skill • I had the training • I did not have the skill •
      I did not have the training

   (C) When I was at the end period of having this job, I felt
      _____ to take on additional tasks
      assigned to me.

      I had the skill • I had the training • I did not have the skill •
      I did have the training

The following questions relate to your awareness of the social rules in each of your jobs

17. The work pace at my job was _____

    fast • relaxed • varied

18. I felt the overall environment of the workplace was _____

    competitive • neutral • cooperative

19. I _____ interacted with my fellow workers on job-related matters.

    very often • often • sometimes • rarely • never

20. Of the people doing a job similar to my own, I had non-job related social relationships with _____ of them.

    all • many • some • very few • none

21. My job _____ involved conferences and meetings.

    very often • not very often • never

22. I _____ interrupted or distracted by others while doing my job.

    was • was not

23. If I was distracted and interrupted, that occurred _____

    constantly • very often • often • not often • rarely

24. My work routine _____ changed.

    constantly • very often • often • was not often • rarely • never

25. I had a chance to access a quiet space _____ while I was working.

    all the time • some of the time • none of the time

26. I had _____ control over my own physical workspace.

    exclusive • a great amount • some control • little control • no control

27. I was sensitive, while performing the tasks of my job, to:

                                    Identify tasks by letter from Question 13, above

  __ Noise   _____

  __ Disturbances in my visual field   _____

  __ Lighting   _____

  __ Odors   _____

  __ Contact and texture (things, people)_____

  __ Tastes and food textures   _____

28. If I was sensitive to certain things, I _____ able to reduce or eliminate the source of my discomfort.

    was • was not

29. If I was uncomfortable, others _____ aware of this.

    were • were not

30. If I was uncomfortable with some sensory events and others were aware of my discomfort, I _____ do something to make them aware.

    did • did not

31. This is what I said or did to make others aware:

32. Even if I said or did nothing to make others aware of my discomfort, they knew anyhow by _____

> observing me • hearing from fellow workers • learning from a supervisor • other (be specific)

33. For this job, _____ originality and creativity was expected of me.

> much • some • no

34. *This question requires an understanding of the cliché* **by the rule**. *This phrase refers to a practice of relying on past practice and written or verbal instructions to specify exactly how a job is to be performed.*

   In my job, my supervisor's attitude about how the job was to be accomplished was that _____ work would be done by the rule.

> all • some • little • no

Your work is evaluated by comparing your work output with that of others doing similar work against known job quality and productivity standards set by others. For many jobs, workers learn about these standards from a variety of sources, but some workers benefit more from one kind of source than the others. Answer the next seven questions by choosing the response which most closely reflected your actual experience.

35. There _____ printed or written quality and productivity standards, which I could read and follow. *(These items include manuals, specification sheets, written samples and written production quotas and schedules. This list is not exhaustive.)*

> were • were not

36. I answered that these materials were available to me. They _____ complete enough for me to really benefit from them.

> were • were not

37. There _____ visual materials depicting quality and productivity standards. *(These items could include signs, charts, step-by-step pictures, graphics and physical samples. This list is not exhaustive.)*

   were • were not

38. I answered that these materials were available to me. They _____ complete enough for me to really benefit from them.

   were • were not

39. I _____ learn of quality and productivity standards through others' spoken instructions to me.

   did • did not

40. I answered that verbal information about quality and standards were available to me. This information _____ complete enough for me to benefit from them.

   was • was not

41. For this job, quality and productivity standards were set by

   _____

   others completely • others and myself • myself

42. Overtime was _____ announced in advance.

   always • sometimes • rarely • never

43. _____ work deadlines were set by others.

   All • Many • Some • Few • No

44. _____ set priorities for my work.

   Others • Others and I • I

45. _____ set the sequence of tasks for my job.

 Others • Others and I • I

46. Compared to others doing the same job, overall, and for long as I was there, I think my performance was _____

 excellent • good • average • poor • bad

47. When I was working there people were _____ recognized and commended for their work.

 always • very often • sometimes • not very often • never

48. My job _____ cause new health problems or worsen an earlier health problem.

 did • did not

49. For my job, I _____ have performance review(s) and evaluation(s).

 did • did not

50. *If you did have evaluations or reviews, write about them briefly in the space below. To help you compose this information, review your job tasks in Question 13 above. Be an honest reporter. Recall the words and phrases used by your reviewers. Their remarks may have touched on other things than just your job performance or the quality of your work. Write three paragraphs, on the beginning, middle period, and final period during which you held the job.*

Probationary period (beginning):

Middle of the job:

End of my job, including exit interview (if any):

The following questions refer to discipline and 'trouble on the job'. As you write your answers, don't get bogged down with self-criticism, and don't report the situation as worse than it really was. The passage of time should have made you more objective about such events, and this part of your employment biography should be written with honesty and a good sense of perspective.

51. I _____ receive warnings or disciplinary actions in the job.

      did • did not

52. I _____ 'frozen' or demoted in the job.

      was • was not

53. If I answered affirmatively to either question above, here are the conditions or behaviors which led up to these measures.

54. Once I became aware of the reasons for my 'freeze', demotion or disciplinary action, I _____ do something to change the conditions of the job or my behaviors.

    did • did not

55. If I did make changes, here is what I did.

56. After I made the changes, I feel that _____

    things got better • things stayed about the same • things got worse • other (be specific)

57. Here is what actually happened after I made the change(s).

58. If I was 'frozen' in my job, demoted or underwent a disciplinary action, **others** _____ make changes to my job or its conditions following those measures.

> did • did not

59. If I answered that others made changes, here is what **they** did.

60. When others made changes to my job or its conditions, I feel that

_____

> things got better • things stayed about the same • things got worse • other (be specific)

61. If things got better, worse or 'other', this is what happened.

62. I held this job for _____ (days, months, or years)

63. This job ended when   _____
    (Choose your answer from   _____
    the following or add your   _____
    own answer. You may choose   _____
    more than one answer.)   _____

    I quit for a better job • I quit for the same type of job • I quit for a
    worse job • the summer ended • the job itself ended (any cause other
    than end of summer job) • I left expecting to be fired or let go • I
    was fired • other (be specific)

*General workplace conditions distinguish one business or institution from another.
These are conditions which executives, managers, and other higher level employees want
to know about when they look for their next job. Many other employees know about
these conditions as well. These conditions contribute to the overall feel of a workplace.
Answer as many of the questions below as you can.*

64. Promotional policies were _____ adhered to.

    always • sometimes • rarely

65. There were _____ power plays and jockeying for favor
    and power.

    very noticeable • somewhat noticeable • not noticeable

66. The boundaries between departments were _____

    very clear • somewhat clear • confused • not clear at all

67. The company had a _____ management style.

    rigid and authoritarian • open and flexible • mixed • other (describe)

68. The company-wide stress, anxiety and tension level was _____

    very high • high • moderate • very low

69. The average employee's knowledge of the general financial health
    of the company was _____

    very good • good • moderate • low • very low

70. Management was _____ open to suggestions.

    very open • moderately open • not open

71. The employees were _____ of management decisions.

    very confident • moderately confident • not confident

*Even though the next two questions read may appear to be simple, your answers to them
indicate the reasons why you feel the job you chose for this period was representative of
your employment during that period.*

72. Here is a brief paragraph describing what I liked about the job.

73. Here is a brief paragraph describing what I didn't like about the job.

Level of Social Skill Understanding   Early Period

74. For each of the items in each job, indicate your level of social skill understanding as reported by others to you. Write an 'X' on the line beneath one of the three choices. Place your response so that your answer will clearly reflect the words of others to you about your understanding and use of that skill. Score yourself on the basis of the remarks of the persons who were very familiar with you at the job.

Good Poor None

A |_____|_____|_____| Greeting and departure phrases, gestures, body language

B |_____|_____|_____| Respect shown to subordinates, equals, and superior

C |_____|_____|_____| Expression of emotions (range and intensity)

D |_____|_____|_____| Awareness of how safe people feel around you

E |_____|_____|_____| Consideration of others

F |_____|_____|_____| Helping others

G |_____|_____|_____| Doing favors (solicited and unsolicited)

H |_____|_____|_____| Offering thanks, praise and recognition to others

I |_____|_____|_____| Expressions of condolence, concern, congratulation

J |_____|_____|_____| Honesty and frankness (candor)

K |_____|_____|_____| Social lies ('white lies')

L |_____|_____|_____| Making up stories which are believable

M |_____|_____|_____| Factual lies

N |_____|_____|_____| Humor (jokes, practical jokes, 'horseplay')

O |_____|_____|_____| Grooming, general appearance, dress, personal hygiene

P |_____|_____|_____| Awareness of physical space of others

Q |_____|_____|_____| Physical contact with others (touching)

R |_____|_____|_____| Eye contact

S |_____|_____|_____| Voice level (modulation)

T |_____|_____|_____| Choice of words and phrases

U |_____|_____|_____| Length of conversation (talking too much or too little)

Good Poor None   **Early Period**

V |_____|_____|_____| Staying on the same topic in conversation
W |_____|_____|_____| Staying on a topic too long in conversation
X |_____|_____|_____| Knowing how to ask for help
Y |_____|_____|_____| Knowing who to ask for help
Z |_____|_____|_____| Knowing when to ask for help

a |_____|_____|_____| Requesting change of conditions and procedures
b |_____|_____|_____| Your response to others' suggestions, criticism, correction
c |_____|_____|_____| When to make suggestions and correction to others
d |_____|_____|_____| How you make suggestions and correction to others
e |_____|_____|_____| Social conversation during work time
f |_____|_____|_____| Social conversation during breaks, lunch, and dinner
g |_____|_____|_____| Discussion of personal friendships and intimate relationships
h |_____|_____|_____| Discussion of personal health problems
i |_____|_____|_____| How your attitude fits in with attitudes of others at work
j |_____|_____|_____| Your choice of work associates, team members and partners
k |_____|_____|_____| Socializing on the job with work associates
l |_____|_____|_____| Socializing off the job with work associates
m |_____|_____|_____| Knowing the unwritten rules for promotion
n |_____|_____|_____| Harassment and abuse
o |_____|_____|_____| Etiquette of reporting problems and making complaints
p |_____|_____|_____| Alerting others about illness, absence, vacation arrangements
q |_____|_____|_____| Interest in voluntarism and community work

SOCIAL SKILLS
(QUESTION 74)

EARLY PERIOD

SOCIAL SKILLS

EARLY PERIOD

SOCIAL SKILLS SUMMARY

EARLY PERIOD

SOCIAL SKILLS

EARLY PERIOD

First Job of Three – *Middle Period*

1. My job title was _____

2. I learned about the job from *(Please circle. You can select more than one answer)*

   advertisement: TV, radio, printed announcement or public notice • job fair • family member or friend • employment counselor; vocational rehabilitation counselor • job placement agency (school placement service, temporary agency) • word of mouth • school or program official • other (be specific)

3. I was hired mainly due to my:

   informal education and training • formal education and training • previous experience in identical or related work • knowing someone inside • referral by a family member or friend • referral by a third party • appearance and presentation in the interview • other (describe)

4. I was:

   employed by others • self-employed • other (describe)

5. I worked mainly:

   outside • inside • in varied locations

6. My hours were _____

   full time • part time (How many hours?) • varied • other (describe)

7. The number of hours I worked were _____

   too many for me at the time • about right for me at the time • too few for me at the time

8. I was paid by _____ *(select one)*

> piecework • commission • salary plus commission • salary • hourly
> wage • barter or scrip • by the job (contract work) • not paid • other
> (describe)

9. I had _____ benefits coverage *(Benefits include unpaid leave,*
vacation, health, dental, retirement, employee discounts, etc.)

> full • some • little • no

10. There was _____ promotion and advancement
opportunity.

> unlimited • some • little • no

11. I thought my pay was _____

> very good • good • adequate • bad • very bad

12. My employer was _____ accommodating when I needed
time away from work, flexible work hours, leaves of absence,
vacation and compensatory time.

> very • somewhat • rarely • never

*On the following pages for Question 13, there are spaces for you to describe each **major** task and responsibility of the job. If you had more tasks than allowed for in the pages in this section of the chapter, duplicate the last page as many times as you need. Add additional letters identifying each new task.*

*After you have identified and described your tasks, further describe the task by indicating how hard the task was to learn and how much of it you learned to do. Use the letters under those questions as shorthand answers. Leave the answering of the questions about how you learned the tasks and how you actually performed them until later. You will return to these two items and complete them when you work through Section 3 on **Learning and Work Styles**.*

13. Job Tasks and Responsibilities

TASK   Learning Difficulty

(A)_____   Hard (H)   Easy (E)

_____

_____   Learned?

_____   Yes (Y)   Partially (P)   No (N)

_____

What I did to learn the task:

How I did the task:

13. Job Tasks and Responsibilities

TASK   Learning Difficulty

(B)_____   Hard (H)   Easy (E)

_____
_____   Learned?

_____   Yes (Y)   Partially (P)   No (N)

_____

What I did to learn the task:

How I did the task:

13. Job Tasks and Responsibilities

TASK   Learning Difficulty

(C)_____   Hard (H)   Easy (E)

_____   Learned?

_____   Yes (Y)   Partially (P)   No (N)

_____

_____

What I did to learn the task:

How I did the task:

13. Job Tasks and Responsibilities

TASK   Learning Difficulty

(D)_____   Hard (H)   Easy (E)

_____

_____   Learned?

_____   Yes (Y)   Partially (P)   No (N)

_____

What I did to learn the task:

How I did the task:

13. Job Tasks and Responsibilities

TASK   Learning Difficulty

(E)_____   Hard (H)   Easy (E)

_____

_____   Learned?

_____   Yes (Y)   Partially (P)   No (N)

_____

What I did to learn the task:

How I did the task:

13. Job Tasks and Responsibilities

TASK   Learning Difficulty

(F)_____   Hard (H)   Easy (E)

_____

_____   Learned?

_____   Yes (Y)   Partially (P)   No (N)

_____

What I did to learn the task:

How I did the task:

13. Job Tasks and Responsibilities

TASK   Learning Difficulty

(G)_____   Hard (H)   Easy (E)

_____   Learned?

_____   Yes (Y)   Partially (P)   No (N)

_____

_____

What I did to learn the task:

How I did the task:

13. Job Tasks and Responsibilities

TASK   Learning Difficulty

(H)_____   Hard (H)   Easy (E)

_____   Learned?

_____   Yes (Y)   Partially (P)   No (N)

_____

_____

What I did to learn the task:

How I did the task:

14. Once I was hired, my training consisted of _____
    (If appropriate, select more than one answer.)

    > formal class training • job and training manuals • formal
    > trainer/mentor • informal trainer/mentor • other (be specific)

15. I made _____ use of my **prior** skills, preparation, training
    and experience in the job?

    > full • partial • little • no

16. *This question relates to your comfort level during three phases of your job, a
    beginning period, a middle period, and the period at the end of the time you held
    the job. For each of these periods, describe additional duties you were given for the
    job, and how prepared you were for the tasks when they were assigned. You may
    choose only two answers for each time. From the answers below, select the answers
    that best describe **your** feeling of readiness for those additional tasks.*

    (A) When I first got the job I felt _____ to take on
        additional tasks assigned to me.

        > I had the skill • I had the training • I did not have the skill •
        > I did not have the training

    (B) After I had gotten used to the job and was in a middle period,
        I felt _____ to take on additional
        tasks assigned to me.

        > I had the skill • I had the training • I did not have the skill •
        > I did not have the training

    (C) When I was at the end period of having this job, I felt
        _____ to take on additional tasks
        assigned to me.

        > I had the skill • I had the training • I did not have the skill •
        > I did have the training

The following questions relate to your awareness of the social rules in each of your jobs

17. The work pace at my job was _____

    fast • relaxed • varied

18. I felt the overall environment of the workplace was _____

    competitive • neutral • cooperative

19. I _____ interacted with my fellow workers on job-related matters.

    very often • often • sometimes • rarely • never

20. Of the people doing a job similar to my own, I had non-job related social relationships with _____ of them.

    all • many • some • very few • none

21. My job _____ involved conferences and meetings.

    very often • not very often • never

22. I _____ interrupted or distracted by others while doing my job.

    was • was not

23. If I was distracted and interrupted, that occurred

    _____

    constantly • very often • often • not often • rarely

24. My work routine _____ changed.

    constantly • very often • often • was not often • rarely • never

25. I had a chance to access a quiet space _____ while I was working.

    all the time • some of the time • none of the time

26. I had _____ control over my own physical workspace.

     exclusive • a great amount • some control • little control • no control

27. I was sensitive, while performing the tasks of my job, to:

Identify tasks by letter from
Question 13, above

__ Noise   _____
__ Disturbances in my visual field   _____
__ Lighting   _____
__ Odors   _____
__ Contact and texture (things, people)_____
__ Tastes and food textures   _____

28. If I was sensitive to certain things, I _____ able to reduce or eliminate the source of my discomfort.

     was • was not

29. If I was uncomfortable, others _____ aware of this.

     were • were not

30. If I was uncomfortable with some sensory events and others were aware of my discomfort, I _____ do something to make them aware.

     did • did not

31. This is what I said or did to make others aware:

32. Even if I said or did nothing to make others aware of my discomfort, they knew anyhow by _____

> observing me • hearing from fellow workers • learning from a supervisor • other (be specific)

33. For this job, _____ originality and creativity was expected of me.

> much • some • no

34. *This question requires an understanding of the cliché **by the rule**. This phrase refers to a practice of relying on past practice and written or verbal instructions to specify exactly how a job is to be performed.*

In my job, my supervisor's attitude about how the job was to be accomplished was that _____ work would be done by the rule.

> all • some • little • no

Your work is evaluated by comparing your work output with that of others doing similar work against known job quality and productivity standards set by others. For many jobs, workers learn about these standards from a variety of sources, but some workers benefit more from one kind of source than the others. Answer the next seven questions by choosing the response which most closely reflected your actual experience.

35. There _____ printed or written quality and productivity standards, which I could read and follow. *(These items include manuals, specification sheets, written samples and written production quotas and schedules. This list is not exhaustive.)*

> were • were not

36. I answered that these materials were available to me. They _____ complete enough for me to really benefit from them.

> were • were not

37. There _____ visual materials depicting quality and productivity standards. *(These items could include signs, charts, step-by-step pictures, graphics and physical samples. This list is not exhaustive.)*

    were • were not

38. I answered that these materials were available to me. They _____ complete enough for me to really benefit from them.

    were • were not

39. I _____ learn of quality and productivity standards through others' spoken instructions to me.

    did • did not

40. I answered that verbal information about quality and standards were available to me. This information _____ complete enough for me to benefit from them.

    was • was not

41. For this job, quality and productivity standards were set by

    _____

    others completely • others and myself • myself

42. Overtime was _____ announced in advance.

    always • sometimes • rarely • never

43. _____ work deadlines were set by others.

    All • Many • Some • Few • No

44. _____ set priorities for my work.

    Others • Others and I • I

45. _____ set the sequence of tasks for my job.

      Others • Others and I • I

46. Compared to others doing the same job, overall, and for long as I was there, I think my performance was _____

      excellent • good • average • poor • bad

47. When I was working there people were _____ recognized and commended for their work.

      always • very often • sometimes • not very often • never

48. My job _____ cause new health problems or worsen an earlier health problem.

      did • did not

49. For my job, I _____ have performance review(s) and evaluation(s).

      did • did not

50. *If you did have evaluations or reviews, write about them briefly in the space below. To help you compose this information, review your job tasks in Question 13 above. Be an honest reporter. Recall the words and phrases used by your reviewers. Their remarks may have touched on other things than just your job performance or the quality of your work. Write three paragraphs, on the beginning, middle period, and final period during which you held the job.*

Probationary period (beginning):

Middle of the job:

End of my job, including exit interview (if any):

The following questions refer to discipline and 'trouble on the job'. As you write your answers, don't get bogged down with self-criticism, and don't report the situation as worse than it really was. The passage of time should have made you more objective about such events, and this part of your employment biography should be written with honesty and a good sense of perspective.

51. I _____ receive warnings or disciplinary actions in the job.

   did • did not

52. I _____ 'frozen' or demoted in the job.

   was • was not

53. If I answered affirmatively to either question above, here are the conditions or behaviors which led up to these measures.

54. Once I became aware of the reasons for my 'freeze', demotion or disciplinary action, I _____ do something to change the conditions of the job or my behaviors.

   did • did not

55. If I did make changes, here is what I did.

56. After I made the changes, I feel that _____

   things got better • things stayed about the same • things got worse • other (be specific)

57. Here is what actually happened after I made the change(s).

58. If I was 'frozen' in my job, demoted or underwent a disciplinary action, **others** _____ make changes to my job or its conditions following those measures.

    did • did not

59. If I answered that others made changes, here is what **they** did.

60. When others made changes to my job or its conditions, I feel that

_____

    things got better • things stayed about the same • things got worse •
other (be specific)

61. If things got better, worse or 'other', this is what happened.

62. I held this job for _____ (days, months, or years)

63. This job ended when   _____
    (Choose your answer from   _____
    the following or add your   _____
    own answer. You may choose   _____
    more than one answer.)   _____

> I quit for a better job • I quit for the same type of job • I quit for a
> worse job • the summer ended • the job itself ended (any cause other
> than end of summer job) • I left expecting to be fired or let go • I
> was fired • other (be specific)

General workplace conditions distinguish one business or institution from another. These are conditions which executives, managers, and other higher level employees want to know about when they look for their next job. Many other employees know about these conditions as well. These conditions contribute to the overall feel of a workplace. Answer as many of the questions below as you can.

64. Promotional policies were _____ adhered to.

> always • sometimes • rarely

65. There were _____ power plays and jockeying for favor
    and power.

> very noticeable • somewhat noticeable • not noticeable

66. The boundaries between departments were _____

> very clear • somewhat clear • confused • not clear at all

67. The company had a _____ management style.

> rigid and authoritarian • open and flexible • mixed • other (describe)

68. The company-wide stress, anxiety and tension level was _____

   very high • high • moderate • very low

69. The average employee's knowledge of the general financial health of the company was _____

   very good • good • moderate • low • very low

70. Management was _____ open to suggestions.

   very open • moderately open • not open

71. The employees were _____ of management decisions.

   very confident • moderately confident • not confident

Even though the next two questions read may appear to be simple, your answers to them indicate the reasons why you feel the job you chose for this period was representative of your employment during that period.

72. Here is a brief paragraph describing what I liked about the job.

73. Here is a brief paragraph describing what I didn't like about the job.

Level of Social Skill Understanding   **Middle Period**

74. For each of the items in each job, indicate your level of social skill understanding as reported by others to you. Write an 'X' on the line beneath one of the three choices. Place your response so that your answer will clearly reflect the words of others to you about your understanding and use of that skill. Score yourself on the basis of the remarks of the persons who were very familiar with you at the job.

Good Poor None

A |_____|_____|_____| Greeting and departure phrases, gestures, body language

B |_____|_____|_____| Respect shown to subordinates, equals, and superior

C |_____|_____|_____| Expression of emotions (range and intensity)

D |_____|_____|_____| Awareness of how safe people feel around you

E |_____|_____|_____| Consideration of others

F |_____|_____|_____| Helping others

G |_____|_____|_____| Doing favors (solicited and unsolicited)

H |_____|_____|_____| Offering thanks, praise and recognition to others

I |_____|_____|_____| Expressions of condolence, concern, congratulation

J |_____|_____|_____| Honesty and frankness (candor)

K |_____|_____|_____| Social lies ('white lies')

L |_____|_____|_____| Making up stories which are believable

M |_____|_____|_____| Factual lies

N |_____|_____|_____| Humor (jokes, practical jokes, 'horseplay')

O |_____|_____|_____| Grooming, general appearance, dress, personal hygiene

P |_____|_____|_____| Awareness of physical space of others

Q |_____|_____|_____| Physical contact with others (touching)

R |_____|_____|_____| Eye contact

S |_____|_____|_____| Voice level (modulation)

T |_____|_____|_____| Choice of words and phrases

U |_____|_____|_____| Length of conversation (talking too much or too little)

	Good	Poor	None	Middle Period
V	|____|____|____|			Staying on the same topic in conversation
W	|____|____|____|			Staying on a topic too long in conversation
X	|____|____|____|			Knowing how to ask for help
Y	|____|____|____|			Knowing who to ask for help
Z	|____|____|____|			Knowing when to ask for help
a	|____|____|____|			Requesting change of conditions and procedures
b	|____|____|____|			Your response to others' suggestions, criticism, correction
c	|____|____|____|			When to make suggestions and correction to others
d	|____|____|____|			How you make suggestions and correction to others
e	|____|____|____|			Social conversation during work time
f	|____|____|____|			Social conversation during breaks, lunch, and dinner
g	|____|____|____|			Discussion of personal friendships and intimate relationships
h	|____|____|____|			Discussion of personal health problems
i	|____|____|____|			How your attitude fits in with attitudes of others at work
j	|____|____|____|			Your choice of work associates, team members and partners
k	|____|____|____|			Socializing on the job with work associates
l	|____|____|____|			Socializing off the job with work associates
m	|____|____|____|			Knowing the unwritten rules for promotion
n	|____|____|____|			Harassment and abuse
o	|____|____|____|			Etiquette of reporting problems and making complaints
p	|____|____|____|			Alerting others about illness, absence, vacation arrangements
q	|____|____|____|			Interest in voluntarism and community work

SOCIAL SKILLS (QUESTION 74)

MIDDLE PERIOD

SOCIAL SKILLS

MIDDLE PERIOD

SOCIAL SKILLS SUMMARY

MIDDLE PERIOD

SOCIAL SKILLS SUMMARY

MIDDLE PERIOD

First Job of Three – *Late Period*

1. My job title was _____

2. I learned about the job from *(Please circle. You can select more than one answer)*

    advertisement: TV, radio, printed announcement or public notice •
    job fair • family member or friend • employment counselor;
    vocational rehabilitation counselor • job placement agency (school
    placement service, temporary agency) • word of mouth • school or
    program official • other (be specific)

3. I was hired mainly due to my:

    informal education and training • formal education and training •
    previous experience in identical or related work • knowing someone
    inside • referral by a family member or friend • referral by a third
    party • appearance and presentation in the interview • other
    (describe)

4. I was:

    employed by others • self-employed • other (describe)

5. I worked mainly:

    outside • inside • in varied locations

6. My hours were _____

    full time • part time (How many hours?) • varied • other (describe)

7. The number of hours I worked were _____

    too many for me at the time • about right for me at the time • too
    few for me at the time

8. I was paid by _____ *(select one)*

> piecework • commission • salary plus commission • salary • hourly
> wage • barter or scrip • by the job (contract work) • not paid • other
> (describe)

9. I had _____ benefits coverage *(Benefits include unpaid leave, vacation, health, dental, retirement, employee discounts, etc.)*

> full • some • little • no

10. There was _____ promotion and advancement opportunity.

> unlimited • some • little • no

11. I thought my pay was _____

> very good • good • adequate • bad • very bad

12. My employer was _____ accommodating when I needed time away from work, flexible work hours, leaves of absence, vacation and compensatory time.

> very • somewhat • rarely • never

*On the following pages for Question 13, there are spaces for you to describe each **major** task and responsibility of the job. If you had more tasks than allowed for in the pages in this section of the chapter, duplicate the last page as many times as you need. Add additional letters identifying each new task.*

*After you have identified and described your tasks, further describe the task by indicating how hard the task was to learn and how much of it you learned to do. Use the letters under those questions as shorthand answers. Leave the answering of the questions about how you learned the tasks and how you actually performed them until later. You will return to these two items and complete them when you work through Section 3 on **Learning and Work Styles**.*

13. Job Tasks and Responsibilities

TASK   Learning Difficulty

(A)_____   Hard (H)   Easy (E)

_____

_____   Learned?

_____

_____   Yes (Y)   Partially (P)   No (N)

_____

What I did to learn the task:

How I did the task:

13. Job Tasks and Responsibilities

TASK

(B)_____

_____

_____

_____

_____

Learning Difficulty

    Hard (H)   Easy (E)

Learned?

    Yes (Y)   Partially (P)   No (N)

What I did to learn the task:

How I did the task:

13. Job Tasks and Responsibilities

TASK   Learning Difficulty

(C)_____   Hard (H)   Easy (E)

_____

_____   Learned?

_____   Yes (Y)   Partially (P)   No (N)

_____

What I did to learn the task:

How I did the task:

13. Job Tasks and Responsibilities

TASK

(D)_____

_____

_____

_____

_____

Learning Difficulty

   Hard (H)   Easy (E)

Learned?

   Yes (Y)   Partially (P)   No (N)

What I did to learn the task:

How I did the task:

13. Job Tasks and Responsibilities

TASK   Learning Difficulty

(E)_____   Hard (H)   Easy (E)

_____

_____   Learned?

_____   Yes (Y)   Partially (P)   No (N)

_____

What I did to learn the task:

How I did the task:

13. Job Tasks and Responsibilities

TASK

(F)_____

_____

_____

_____

_____

Learning Difficulty

   Hard (H)   Easy (E)

Learned?

   Yes (Y)   Partially (P)   No (N)

What I did to learn the task:

How I did the task:

13. Job Tasks and Responsibilities

TASK   Learning Difficulty

(G)_____   Hard (H)   Easy (E)

_____
_____   Learned?

_____   Yes (Y)   Partially (P)   No (N)

_____

What I did to learn the task:

How I did the task:

13. Job Tasks and Responsibilities

TASK   Learning Difficulty

(H)_____   Hard (H)   Easy (E)

_____

_____   Learned?

_____   Yes (Y)   Partially (P)   No (N)

_____

What I did to learn the task:

How I did the task:

14. Once I was hired, my training consisted of _____
    (If appropriate, select more than one answer.)

    > formal class training • job and training manuals • formal
    > trainer/mentor • informal trainer/mentor • other (be specific)

15. I made _____ use of my **prior** skills, preparation, training
    and experience in the job?

    > full • partial • little • no

16. *This question relates to your comfort level during three phases of your job, a
    beginning period, a middle period, and the period at the end of the time you held
    the job. For each of these periods, describe additional duties you were given for the
    job, and how prepared you were for the tasks when they were assigned. You may
    choose only two answers for each time. From the answers below, select the answers
    that best describe **your** feeling of readiness for those additional tasks.*

    (A) When I first got the job I felt _____ to take on
        additional tasks assigned to me.

        > I had the skill • I had the training • I did not have the skill •
        > I did not have the training

    (B) After I had gotten used to the job and was in a middle period,
        I felt _____ to take on additional
        tasks assigned to me.

        > I had the skill • I had the training • I did not have the skill •
        > I did not have the training

    (C) When I was at the end period of having this job, I felt
        _____ to take on additional tasks
        assigned to me.

        > I had the skill • I had the training • I did not have the skill •
        > I did have the training

The following questions relate to your awareness of the social rules in each of your jobs

17. The work pace at my job was _____

    fast • relaxed • varied

18. I felt the overall environment of the workplace was _____

    competitive • neutral • cooperative

19. I _____ interacted with my fellow workers on job-related matters.

    very often • often • sometimes • rarely • never

20. Of the people doing a job similar to my own, I had non-job related social relationships with _____ of them.

    all • many • some • very few • none

21. My job _____ involved conferences and meetings.

    very often • not very often • never

22. I _____ interrupted or distracted by others while doing my job.

    was • was not

23. If I was distracted and interrupted, that occurred

    _____

    constantly • very often • often • not often • rarely

24. My work routine _____ changed.

    constantly • very often • often • was not often • rarely • never

25. I had a chance to access a quiet space _____ while I was working.

    all the time • some of the time • none of the time

26. I had _____ control over my own physical workspace.

   exclusive • a great amount • some control • little control • no control

27. I was sensitive, while performing the tasks of my job, to:

   Identify tasks by letter from
   Question 13, above

   __ Noise   _____
   __ Disturbances in my visual field   _____
   __ Lighting   _____
   __ Odors   _____
   __ Contact and texture (things, people)_____
   __ Tastes and food textures   _____

28. If I was sensitive to certain things, I _____ able to reduce or eliminate the source of my discomfort.

   was • was not

29. If I was uncomfortable, others _____ aware of this.

   were • were not

30. If I was uncomfortable with some sensory events and others were aware of my discomfort, I _____ do something to make them aware.

   did • did not

31. This is what I said or did to make others aware:

32. Even if I said or did nothing to make others aware of my discomfort, they knew anyhow by _____

> observing me • hearing from fellow workers • learning from a supervisor • other (be specific)

33. For this job, _____ originality and creativity was expected of me.

> much • some • no

34. *This question requires an understanding of the cliché **by the rule**. This phrase refers to a practice of relying on past practice and written or verbal instructions to specify exactly how a job is to be performed.*

In my job, my supervisor's attitude about how the job was to be accomplished was that _____ work would be done by the rule.

> all • some • little • no

Your work is evaluated by comparing your work output with that of others doing similar work against known job quality and productivity standards set by others. For many jobs, workers learn about these standards from a variety of sources, but some workers benefit more from one kind of source than the others. Answer the next seven questions by choosing the response which most closely reflected your actual experience.

35. There _____ printed or written quality and productivity standards, which I could read and follow. *(These items include manuals, specification sheets, written samples and written production quotas and schedules. This list is not exhaustive.)*

> were • were not

36. I answered that these materials were available to me. They _____ complete enough for me to really benefit from them.

> were • were not

37. There _____ visual materials depicting quality and productivity standards. *(These items could include signs, charts, step-by-step pictures, graphics and physical samples. This list is not exhaustive.)*

    were • were not

38. I answered that these materials were available to me. They _____ complete enough for me to really benefit from them.

    were • were not

39. I _____ learn of quality and productivity standards through others' spoken instructions to me.

    did • did not

40. I answered that verbal information about quality and standards were available to me. This information _____ complete enough for me to benefit from them.

    was • was not

41. For this job, quality and productivity standards were set by

    _____

    others completely • others and myself • myself

42. Overtime was _____ announced in advance.

    always • sometimes • rarely • never

43. _____ work deadlines were set by others.

    All • Many • Some • Few • No

44. _____ set priorities for my work.

    Others • Others and I • I

45. _____ set the sequence of tasks for my job.

    Others • Others and I • I

46. Compared to others doing the same job, overall, and for long as I was there, I think my performance was _____

    excellent • good • average • poor • bad

47. When I was working there people were _____ recognized and commended for their work.

    always • very often • sometimes • not very often • never

48. My job _____ cause new health problems or worsten an earlier health problem.

    did • did not

49. For my job, I _____ have performance review(s) and evaluation(s).

    did • did not

50. *If you did have evaluations or reviews, write about them briefly in the space below. To help you compose this information, review your job tasks in Question 13 above. Be an honest reporter. Recall the words and phrases used by your reviewers. Their remarks may have touched on other things than just your job performance or the quality of your work. Write three paragraphs, on the beginning, middle period, and final period during which you held the job.*

Probationary period (beginning):

Middle of the job:

End of my job, including exit interview (if any):

The following questions refer to discipline and 'trouble on the job'. As you write your answers, don't get bogged down with self-criticism, and don't report the situation as worse than it really was. The passage of time should have made you more objective about such events, and this part of your employment biography should be written with honesty and a good sense of perspective.

51. I _____ receive warnings or disciplinary actions in the job.

    did • did not

52. I _____ 'frozen' or demoted in the job.

    was • was not

53. If I answered affirmatively to either question above, here are the conditions or behaviors which led up to these measures.

54. Once I became aware of the reasons for my 'freeze', demotion or disciplinary action, I _____ do something to change the conditions of the job or my behaviors.

   did • did not

55. If I did make changes, here is what I did.

56. After I made the changes, I feel that _____

   things got better • things stayed about the same • things got worse • other (be specific)

57. Here is what actually happened after I made the change(s).

58. If I was 'frozen' in my job, demoted or underwent a disciplinary action, **others** _____ make changes to my job or its conditions following those measures.

  did • did not

59. If I answered that others made changes, here is what **they** did.

60. When others made changes to my job or its conditions, I feel that

  _____

  things got better • things stayed about the same • things got worse • other (be specific)

61. If things got better, worse or 'other', this is what happened.

62. I held this job for _____ (days, months, or years)

63. This job ended when   _____
    (Choose your answer from   _____
    the following or add your _____
    own answer. You may choose _____
    more than one answer.)   _____

> I quit for a better job • I quit for the same type of job • I quit for a
> worse job • the summer ended • the job itself ended (any cause other
> than end of summer job) • I left expecting to be fired or let go • I
> was fired • other (be specific)

*General workplace conditions distinguish one business or institution from another.
These are conditions which executives, managers, and other higher level employees want
to know about when they look for their next job. Many other employees know about
these conditions as well. These conditions contribute to the overall feel of a workplace.
Answer as many of the questions below as you can.*

64. Promotional policies were _____ adhered to.

> always • sometimes • rarely

65. There were _____ power plays and jockeying for favor
    and power.

> very noticeable • somewhat noticeable • not noticeable

66. The boundaries between departments were _____

> very clear • somewhat clear • confused • not clear at all

67. The company had a _____ management style.

> rigid and authoritarian • open and flexible • mixed • other (describe)

68. The company-wide stress, anxiety and tension level was _____

    very high • high • moderate • very low

69. The average employee's knowledge of the general financial health of the company was _____

    very good • good • moderate • low • very low

70. Management was _____ open to suggestions.

    very open • moderately open • not open

71. The employees were _____ of management decisions.

    very confident • moderately confident • not confident

Even though the next two questions read may appear to be simple, your answers to them indicate the reasons why you feel the job you chose for this period was representative of your employment during that period.

72. Here is a brief paragraph describing what I liked about the job.

73. Here is a brief paragraph describing what I didn't like about the job.

Level of Social Skill Understanding   Late Period

74. For each of the items in each job, indicate your level of social skill understanding as reported by others to you. Write an 'X' on the line beneath one of the three choices. Place your response so that your answer will clearly reflect the words of others to you about your understanding and use of that skill. Score yourself on the basis of the remarks of the persons who were very familiar with you at the job.

Good Poor None

A |_____|_____|_____| Greeting and departure phrases, gestures, body language

B |_____|_____|_____| Respect shown to subordinates, equals, and superior

C |_____|_____|_____| Expression of emotions (range and intensity)

D |_____|_____|_____| Awareness of how safe people feel around you

E |_____|_____|_____| Consideration of others

F |_____|_____|_____| Helping others

G |_____|_____|_____| Doing favors (solicited and unsolicited)

H |_____|_____|_____| Offering thanks, praise and recognition to others

I |_____|_____|_____| Expressions of condolence, concern, congratulation

J |_____|_____|_____| Honesty and frankness (candor)

K |_____|_____|_____| Social lies ('white lies')

L |_____|_____|_____| Making up stories which are believable

M |_____|_____|_____| Factual lies

N |_____|_____|_____| Humor (jokes, practical jokes, 'horseplay')

O |_____|_____|_____| Grooming, general appearance, dress, personal hygiene

P |_____|_____|_____| Awareness of physical space of others

Q |_____|_____|_____| Physical contact with others (touching)

R |_____|_____|_____| Eye contact

S |_____|_____|_____| Voice level (modulation)

T |_____|_____|_____| Choice of words and phrases

U |_____|_____|_____| Length of conversation (talking too much or too little)

Good Poor None   **Late Period**

V |_____|_____|_____| Staying on the same topic in conversation

W |_____|_____|_____| Staying on a topic too long in conversation

X |_____|_____|_____| Knowing how to ask for help

Y |_____|_____|_____| Knowing who to ask for help

Z |_____|_____|_____| Knowing when to ask for help

a |_____|_____|_____| Requesting change of conditions and procedures

b |_____|_____|_____| Your response to others' suggestions, criticism, correction

c |_____|_____|_____| When to make suggestions and correction to others

d |_____|_____|_____| How you make suggestions and correction to others

e |_____|_____|_____| Social conversation during work time

f |_____|_____|_____| Social conversation during breaks, lunch, and dinner

g |_____|_____|_____| Discussion of personal friendships and intimate relationships

h |_____|_____|_____| Discussion of personal health problems

i |_____|_____|_____| How your attitude fits in with attitudes of others at work

j |_____|_____|_____| Your choice of work associates, team members and partners

k |_____|_____|_____| Socializing on the job with work associates

l |_____|_____|_____| Socializing off the job with work associates

m |_____|_____|_____| Knowing the unwritten rules for promotion

n |_____|_____|_____| Harassment and abuse

o |_____|_____|_____| Etiquette of reporting problems and making complaints

p |_____|_____|_____| Alerting others about illness, absence, vacation arrangements

q |_____|_____|_____| Interest in voluntarism and community work

SOCIAL SKILLS (QUESTION 74)

LATE PERIOD

SOCIAL SKILLS

LATE PERIOD

SOCIAL SKILLS SUMMARY

LATE PERIOD

SOCIAL SKILLS
SUMMARY

LATE PERIOD

SECTION 3

LEARNING AND WORK STYLES (QUESTION 13)

EARLY PERIOD

LEARNING AND WORK STYLES

EARLY PERIOD

LEARNING AND WORK STYLES

MIDDLE PERIOD

LEARNING AND WORK STYLES

MIDDLE PERIOD

LEARNING AND WORK STYLES

LATE PERIOD

LEARNING AND WORK STYLES

LATE PERIOD

LEARNING AND WORK STYLES

SUMMARY: HOW I LEARN

LEARNING AND WORK STYLES

SUMMARY: HOW I WORK

SECTION 4

INTERESTS, SKILLS AND TALENTS MASTER LIST

INTERESTS, SKILLS AND TALENTS MASTER LIST

INTERESTS, SKILLS AND TALENTS

EARLY PERIOD

INTERESTS, SKILLS AND TALENTS

MIDDLE PERIOD

INTERESTS, SKILLS AND TALENTS

LATE PERIOD

SECTION 5

MY WORK
AND ASPERGER SYNDROME

EARLY PERIOD

MY WORK
AND ASPERGER SYNDROME

EARLY PERIOD

MY WORK
AND ASPERGER SYNDROME

MIDDLE PERIOD

MY WORK
AND ASPERGER SYNDROME

MIDDLE PERIOD

MY WORK
AND ASPERGER SYNDROME

LATE PERIOD

MY WORK
AND ASPERGER SYNDROME
SUMMARY

MY WORK
AND ASPERGER SYNDROME
MY CONCLUSIONS

SECTION 6

PERSONAL TOOLS
AND STRATEGIES
MASTER LIST

PERSONAL TOOLS AND STRATEGIES MASTER LIST

PERSONAL TOOLS
AND STRATEGIES
MASTER LIST

PERSONAL TOOLS
AND STRATEGIES
MASTER LIST

PERSONAL TOOLS AND STRATEGIES MASTER LIST

EARLY PERIOD

PERSONAL TOOLS AND STRATEGIES MASTER LIST

MIDDLE PERIOD

PERSONAL TOOLS AND STRATEGIES MASTER LIST

LATE PERIOD

PERSONAL TOOLS AND STRATEGIES TOOL MAINTENANCE AND CHECK-UP LIST

PERSONAL TOOLS AND STRATEGIES TOOL MAINTENANCE AND CHECK-UP LIST

SECTION 7

Diagnosis, Disclosure and Self-Advocacy

Questions 75–101

75. What led you to seek a diagnosis from others or diagnose yourself? Describe the incident, the person(s) suggesting diagnosis, and what was going on in your life at the time.

76. Recall the first time you told another person about your diagnosis. Describe the situation. Consider the following items to be included in to your answer.

   - *Who did you tell?*
   - *What led up to your disclosure?*
   - *Were you in a situation where you 'had' to reveal your AS?*
   - *How much information about AS did you provide them?*
   - *How comfortable did you feel revealing the information?*

77. Describe what happened with you after your disclosure. Mention the other person's response, but do not dwell on that. This question refers to your reactions following that event.

78. How many people do you consider close to you? Write a number.

79. Was the person to whom you first revealed your diagnosis a person close to you?

    Yes • No

80. Regardless of your answer above, are there others close to you who do not know of your diagnosis?

    Yes • No

81. If your answer to Question 80 is 'Yes', why have you not told them? Be specific. Start by describing each person's relationship to you.

82. In any job since your diagnosis, did you tell fellow workers about your diagnosis?

Yes • No

83. If other workers know about your AS, did you seek them out to tell them more?

Yes • No

84. Review the guide items in Question 76, above, referring to a description of the first time you revealed your diagnosis to anyone. Review Question 77, above, which asks you how you felt afterward. Write a paragraph describing those same items as they applied to your disclosure to others at work.

85. Has anyone other than yourself revealed your diagnosis to others?

Yes • No

86. If you answered 'Yes', who did that?

87. Why was the disclosure made?

88. Did they discuss they would be disclosing your diagnosis to someone else before doing it?

Yes • No

89. If they did discuss informing others about your diagnosis with you, did you agree to it?

Yes • No

90. If they discussed disclosure with you, and you agreed, did they inform you about how that would be done? (Who, when, where, and how much information they intended to reveal)

Yes, they went over everything completely • Yes, but some things were not completely explained • Yes, but their explanation was inadequate • No

91. Did they ask you share your thoughts about what they were about to do?

Yes • No

92. If you told them of any reservations or suggested things they should not share with others, did you feel they understood what you said?

    Yes • No

93. Did they agree to observe any conditions you set about their disclosure to others?

    Yes • No

94. Did they honor their promise?

    Yes • No

95. How satisfied were you with the results of their action?

96. If AS affected your employment in the past, following your diagnosis did you tell your employer about your AS?

    Yes • No

97. If your answer is 'No', describe why you did not inform your employer.

98. If you or others informed your employer about your AS, have either of you discussed accommodations or other arrangements to reduce job stress?

    Yes • No

99. If accommodation was not discussed, do you think your employer was open to talking about this matter later?

    Yes • No

100. If accommodations were discussed, write about who proposed them and what they were.

101. If you revealed your AS to your employer, what effect did that have on your feelings about job security? Describe those feelings both before and after as best you can.

DIAGNOSIS, DICLOSURE AND SELF-ADVOCACY

REFLECTIONS ON MY DISCLOSURE EXPERIENCES

DIAGNOSIS, DICLOSURE AND SELF-ADVOCACY

REFLECTIONS ON MY DISCLOSURE EXPERIENCES

SECTION 8

MY WISH LIST
QUESTIONS FOR THE FUTURE

- What are 'my'mistakes I can learn from?
- Is there a simple fix I could bring to a complex problem?
- Can I break a challenge down into steps?
- Who can I talk with?
- What good parts of my jobs can I combine into a 'custom job'?
- Here is what I do to get 're-charged:'
- What kinds of questions should I ask of a helping professional?
- Can I trade a skill I'm not using on the job for one I don't have?
- Is there room for promotion or advancement in my work? Do I want it?
- Are my leisure time interests and recreation in balance?
- Is there someone at work I can share small concerns with?
- Does my spouse (mate, partner) understand my AS challenges I face at work?
- Is there a support group for adults with AS in my community?
- Could I 'start' a support group?
- Could I barter some of my skills in exchange for training in skills I don't have?
- How much money do I need to live on? What are my long term goals for income?
- Is there subsidized training available for job skills I need to acquire?
- Do I dare have myself videotaped for mock interviews or mock disclosure?
- What are my 'scripts' that I use after I lose my temper? Do they work?

MY WISH LIST
QUESTIONS FOR THE FUTURE

- With whom can I practice 'asking for help'?
- Do any of my interests have an income-producing potential?
- What do I do on vacations?
- How do I ask others if they agree with the way I see things?
- Do I regularly 'check in' with others to see whether they are following me in my conversations with them?
- Can I give myself a compliment?
- How do I act when I am depressed?
- Can I use other means to organize my work? Who can I ask about this?
- Do I have problems with time? If I do, how do I handle them?
- Have I ever listened to myself from a tape recording of my conversation?
- Would I be interested in doing that? Why or why not?
- Do I have public 'grooming habits' that I could alter?
- How do I monitor my emotions? Or do I?
- How do I ask questions of people?
- Do I ask questions of people?
- How do I find out my true worth as a worker?
- How do I offer criticism to others?
- Is there assistive technology that would make my work easier?
- If I'm really good at something, how do I turn down offers of being a manager?
- How do I teach someone to do what I do?

MY WISH LIST
QUESTIONS FOR THE FUTURE

- How do I explain how I learn something to a stranger?
- Do I know where my 'personal space' boundaries are? How do I explain them to others?
- Do I want to know something more about my body language and facial expressions?

WRITE YOUR OWN QUESTIONS HERE

MY WISH LIST
NOTES TO MYSELF

MY WISH LIST
NOTES TO MYSELF

Asperger Syndrome Characteristics

Below is a list of Asperger Syndrome (AS) characteristics. This list is not intended for diagnostic use. These items were extracted from medical diagnostic criteria, descriptions offered by medical and counseling professionals and , articles by educators, as well as from the biographies of over 75 independent living, medically or self-diagnosed AS adults over the age of 25. While every adult occasionally manifests these characteristics, what distinguishes these characteristics for AS adults are their consistency of appearance, intensity, and the sheer number of them appearing simultaneously. This list is not exhaustive. The author requests that readers wishing to write their employment biographies add no additional manifestations, characteristics, or behaviors to the list.

Some behavior characteristics may not apply to everyone, so persons consulting this list should not feel compelled to identify with all of them. Some of these manifestations also appear contradictory: bear in mind that their intensity, consistency and continuance occur in situations which otherwise do not seem to warrant the behaviors. AS adults composing employment biographies for themselves should exercise good judgment and weigh the influence of these AS manifestations as they apply only to their work lives.

The list is divided into four parts:

- physical manifestations
- work characteristics
- cognitive characteristics
- social characteristics.

Physical manifestations

- Difficulties with balance; unusual gait, stance and posture
- Gross or fine motor coordination problems
- Stims (self-stimulatory behavior serving to reduce anxiety, stress or express pleasure)

- Self-Injurious (SI) or disfiguring behaviors; nail biting
- Monotone vocal expression; limited range of inflection
- Difficulty monitoring and controlling voice level
- Echolalia (repetition of certain sounds, words or phrases)
- Verbosity
- Difficulty with initiating and maintaining eye contact
- Failure to observe the personal physical space of others
- Strong food preferences and aversions
- Limited food choices; unusual and rigid eating behaviors and routines
- Limited clothing preferences
- Hypersensitivity to certain sounds, odors, colors and lighting, tactile and touch, stimuli, taste and food textures
- Bad personal hygiene and self-care
- Concentration and attention problems
- Chronic sleep problems
- Depression
- Anxiety
- Low apparent sexual interest
- Low sensivity to heat, cold, and/or pain.

Work characteristics

- Difficulty with teamwork
- Discomfort with competition; out of scale reaction to losing
- Difficulty in handling relationships with authority figures
- Difficulty in receiving and giving criticism and correction
- Reluctance to accept positions of authority and supervision
- Low level of assertiveness
- Reluctance to ask for help or support
- Difficulty in negotiating conflict situations or being an effective self-advocate
- Problem accepting compliments, often responding with self-deprecating or quizzical comments
- Sarcasm, negativism, unsolicited criticism
- Deliberate withholding of peak performance due to belief that best efforts may be unacknowledged, unrewarded, or appropriated by others
- Perfectionism
- Great concern about order and appearance of personal work area

- Difficulty in remembering where items used moments before are located
- Low awareness of danger to self or others
- Slow or substandard performance
- Difficulty with starting projects
- Daydreaming
- Attention to detail
- Unorthodox work routines
- Enjoyment of routine or 'mindless', repetitive tasks
- Strong reactions to changes in persons, environment, or work conditions
- Stress reaction to multi-tasking, change of priorities and conflict of priorities
- Low motivation to perform tasks of no immediate personal interest
- Unpleasant reactions to distraction and interruption
- Difficulty with writing and making reports
- Strong discomfort with unstructured time
- Avoid 'hanging out' or small talk on and off the job
- Anxiety about performance and acceptance, despite recognition and commendation
- Punctual in attendance
- Conscientious about completing tasks

Cognitive characteristics

Communication

- Stilted or pedantic conversation style ('The Professor')
- Poor understanding of the reciprocal rules of speech: interrupting others, lengthy monologues, dominating/controlling conversation, intervention timing difficulty, trouble with shifting topics, subject perseveration, minimum or no participation in conversation where participation is expected, problems initiating and terminating conversation; difficulty in repairing conversations
- Literal interpretation of words
- Literal interpretation of instructions or directions
- Difficulty understanding the meaning of colloquial phrases, clichés, and humorous remarks
- Low awareness of non-verbal conversational cues of others (stance, posture and subtle facial expressions).

Learning

- Preference for visually oriented training and instruction
- Good response to Sensory Integration (SI) and Auditory Integration Therapy (AIT)
- Preference for tactile, hands-on learning
- Preference for rote instruction
- Preference for step by step instruction with practice of each step before proceeding to the next step
- Preference for simple incremental steps without intervening global explanations or conceptual information
- Agitation with instructions that assume knowledge and delete or otherwise skip steps
- Dependence on routine and clear rules
- Concrete thinking
- Repetitive questions
- Excessive questions
- Highly susceptible to distractions and interruptions
- Reluctance to ask for help: knowing when, who, why, and how to ask for help
- Difficulty clearly expressing a problem
- Unorthodox methods or solutions to problems
- Extreme reaction to failure to solve problems
- Poor performance on some standardized tests where conventional methods of response is required
- Low motivation to learn subject matter of no personal interest
- Low threshold for certain kinds of sensory overload
- Difficulty with the physical act of writing
- Difficulty in learning self-started relaxation and recreational release behaviors.

Thought

- Limited range of highly developed interests
- Difficulty with short-term memory
- Exceptional long-term memory
- Lack of 'common sense'
- Impulsiveness

- Global mental shutdown during periods of sensory overload or extreme stress
- 'Flat' affect
- Difficulty identifying and differentiating own emotions and expressing them
- Difficulty with self-monitoring of emotions
- Black and white thinking
- Difficulty understanding broad concepts due to getting lost in the details (the tree/forest problem)
- Difficulty understanding rules for games of social entertainment
- Difficulty imagining thoughts of others in the same setting (theory of mind issues)
- Difficulty with understanding that others' thoughts may be different than one's own
- Assuming others can read one's mind without expressing one's own thoughts through words or behavior
- Missing or misunderstanding the meaning of others' agendas, priorities or preferences, words or behaviors.

Executive function issues

- Difficulty understanding the relationship between a personal action and its consequence
- Difficulty drawing relationships between an event and an overarching concept
- Problem combining both facts and ideas (some contradictory) into a grander schema
- Difficulty assessing the relative importance of details
- Dropping details
- Difficulty in establishing priorities
- Poor estimation of time required to complete a task, even if the task has been performed frequently in the past
- Difficulty with organizing and sequencing (planning, execution and successful completion of tasks in a logical, functional order)
- Difficulty stopping non-functional, irrelevant routines despite intellectual awareness of their dysfunction
- Poor judgment of when a task is finished
- Messy and disorganized appearance of work area.

Social characteristics

- Difficulty in perceiving and applying unwritten social rules
- Rigid adherence to rules or social conventions where flexibility is desired
- Scrupulous honesty and frankness directly expressed with little or no tact
- Immature manners
- 'In your own world'
- 'Loner'
- Great concern for personal privacy
- Serious all the time
- Strange or apparent lack of sense of humor
- Shyness
- Difficulty with reciprocal displays of greetings and social pleasantries
- Discomfort with manipulating or 'playing games' with others
- High sensitivity to injustice
- Difficulty adopting a social mask to obscure real feelings, moods, and reactions
- Using social masks inappropriately (I am 'X' while everyone else is 'Y')
- Excessive talk; frequent problem focusing exclusively on self-involved interests or topics
- Apparent low level of recreational, public relaxation or 'time out' activities
- Blunt emotional expression
- Difficulty with trust issues: naïve trust in others, problems forming acquaintanceships, friendships and intimate relationships, difficulty in distinguishing between acquaintanceship and friendship, poor understanding of boundaries in relationships
- Constant level of paranoia or vigilance
- Poorly concealed self-anger, anger and resentment toward others
- Pouting, ruminating and fixating on bad experiences with people or events for an inordinate length of time
- Flash temper
- Tantrums, rages, shut-down and self-isolating behaviors appearing 'out of nowhere'.

Internet Website Addresses

All of these references are Internet addresses. Information for the general public about Asperger Syndrome is being developed too swiftly to remain confined to only hard-copy print. Until very recently, there was a true shortage of literature on high functioning adult issues, except for what was covered in the literature about children and adolescents. Even in the current literature, adult issues are covered almost as an afterthought.

The list of websites presented here is selective. Most of them are lodestone sites. Some are important for historical reasons, yet are current and very heavily visited. These are sites that contain a high number of links to other sites. Unlike many smaller, personal or organizational websites, these sites are not ephemeral. Smaller, private websites are often in place today but move or disappear tomorrow. Maintaining a stable website on a reliable server is a major job.

Many of these sites have pages and features that are under constant construction, upgrading, and updating. You may not be able to access all of their features at any given time. Others may not be accessible by a particular browser. In your searches if you keep seeing a '404' error, which means that the website is not accessible or to be found by one browser, try another browser. By using both of the major browsers, Microsoft's Internet Explorer and Netscape/AOL's Navigator and Communicator, you should be able to access all sites, if they are still 'up'. If you are using old, slow equipment, you may be able to set your browser to receive just text. By choosing that option, your downloads will be faster. Unless otherwise indicated, all websites below are accessed using the regular Hyper Text Transfer Protocol (http://). Website addresses – Universal Resource Locators (URLs) – are case-sensitive. Be mindful of capital letters, punctuation marks and spacing. Website addresses do not use empty spaces.

Meta sites

Welcome to dogpile

This is a multi-search engine website for eleven major search engines. It is convenient because a single search entry gives the surfer access to eleven search engines. There are other independent search engines that are very powerful, but the convenience of having this many at one site may be attractive to first-time surfers.

http://www.dogpile.com

OASIS (Online Asperger Syndrome Information and Support)

The 'Grandmother' site for AS maintained by Barbara Kirby. This site has links galore and many embedded articles. Barbara's website also introduces the surfer to the Asperger Webring, a growing number of websites maintained by parents of AS children and persons with AS.

http://www.udel.edu/bkirby/asperger/

Tourette's Syndrome 'Rage Attacks' page of Leslie Packer, PhD

One of the greatest challenges for adults with AS is management of our anger. Many children and AS adults have a 'touch' of Tourette's Syndrome. Leslie Packer is a clinical psychologist who is also a superb special education advocate. This article on rage attacks is a must-read for adults on the spectrum as well as anyone else interested in the devastating effects of our anger.

http://www.tourettesyndrome.net/rage.htm

Tony Attwood

Dr Attwood maintains a small but powerful website. In addition to articles he has written, his site contains an excellent list of current research materials. His work with adults is on the cutting edge. Below his website I include the location of the transcripts of two all-day conferences held in England with spouses of AS partners. The first transcript requires the reader to have Adobe Acrobat reader on their computer. That reader is available free of charge from Adobe at the following URL: *http://www.adobe.com/products/acrobat/readstep2.html*.

http://www.tonyattwood.com/
http://www.oneworld.org/autism_uk/family/partner.html
http://www.faaas.org/transcripts/coventry.html

Nancy Mandel's Dallas website

Besides being a mother of a youngster with Asperger Syndrome, Nancy Mandel is a reading specialist and special education advocate. She is also a 'URL junkie', which is our good fortune. Although many of the websites linked to her page deal with special education and learning disabilities, she has some good links for adult issues.

http://www.dallasasperger.org/

Families of Adults Afflicted with Asperger Syndrome (FAAAS)

Despite its incendiary title, this website is a sound introduction to the response of the 'other halves' of marriages where one spouse is on the autistic spectrum and the other is not. Since his appearance in Coventry in May 2000, Dr Attwood has begun a round of appearances at conferences to discuss the issues raised by spouses not on the spectrum married to those who are on it.

http://www.faaas.org/

'Oops... Wrong Planet! Syndrome'

This site is maintained by a high functioning autistic mom motivated by her son's AS. Janet Norman-Baine keeps one of the largest constantly upgraded lists of links on the Internet. She has embedded an enormous number of articles in her Web page.

http://www.isn.net/~jypsy/

Independent living on the autistic spectrum (InLv)

This is the website of Martijn Dekker, a gifted Dutch young AS adult who has numerous projects going on simultaneously. This site contains original articles written by members of the private, closed Email InLv list. It has excellent links to other articles embedded in the On The Same Page (OTSP) website, which is an older website slowly dying of neglect. InLv is a listserv with numerous special topic forums. It is a very active and robust list. Martijn has contact information posted for AS persons interested in joining this exclusive listserv.

http://www.inlv.demon.nl

Autism network international

This site is maintained by several list owners. Like Martijn Dekker's InLv listserv, it is open to adults on the autistic spectrum and 'autistic cousins'. Postings have a 'different flavor' than those on InLv. It is also open to parents of children on the spectrum, but postings of members must address a specific forum and follow the etiquette established by the list owners. It has an active Email subscription listserv, which means the postings are not available to the general public. ANI sponsors an annual convention and camp experience just for autistic individuals and their families.

http://www.ani.ac

New horizons for learning

Dee Dickinson, the owner of this website, has collected more information on promising and best practices in adult learning of any other website I could find. The layout of the website is superb, and especially appreciated by visually-oriented persons. Articles featured make common sense and do not patronize the reader.

http://www.newhorizons.org/

LDonline

This is a site sponsored partially by WETA-TV in Washington DC. It is among the richest of sources for articles on learning disabilities. Its 'LD in Depth' section contains a cornucopia of well-written archived articles, and is constantly being augmented.

http://ldonline.org/

NLDline

This is Sue Thompson's webpage. Articles, links, references to research, promising and best practices of learning communication and social skills abound here.

http://www.nldline.com

Learning Disabilities Association of California

Each state in the US has chapters of the national organization, but this chapter is something special. Articles on its webpage are far-reaching and hard-hitting. Articles on Nonverbal Learning Disorders by author Sue Thompson, MA, are particularly valuable. Although the website is geared to K-12 education, many trainers and teachers of adults have adopted practices mentioned in articles here.

http://www.ldaca.org/

Assistive and adaptive computing technology in special education

Don't let the title fool you. This website contains an enormous amount of information on US special education and advocacy, but as you scroll down the list of links, you will see many links to information on all kinds of disabilities, best educational practices for children (and adults), detailed information on assistive technology for learners of all ages and more. Annie Macleod, the webmistress, is one of the fastest 'hands' in the business to post current information on topics dealing with disabilities, advocacy, and learning.

http://at-advocacy.philly.com/index.html

Educational Resources Information Center (ERIC)

This is the major US clearinghouse for special educational materials. Although oriented towards K-12, the US Department of Education and a number of other major organizational players contribute boxes of articles to be accessed through archives on this one prime location. The editors of this service are on the constant lookout for new contributions and articles. There are substantial offerings on learning disabilities and adult education. The address below is the home page, maintained by servers at Syracuse University in New York State.

http://www.askeric.org/

NICHCY (National Information Center for Children and Youth with Disabilities)

This organization is tightly connected with the US Department of Education, Office of Special Education Programs. Of special value is its 'Publications' link. It also has good information about disability services and organizations in each state in the US.

http://nichcy.org/

Medline

This is the open-sesame search engine address for listing of millions of medical and psychology articles in professional journals. Many listed articles have abstracts published on this website. The site is maintained by the National Library of Medicine at the National Institutes of Health in Washington, DC.

Access became free to the general public only recently.

http://www.ncbi.nlm.nih.gov/PubMed/

Thomas

This is the search engine for the US Congress. Although it is principally designed for current events, you can surf for copies of relevant US laws, Congressional Committee Reports and Congressional Record contents.

Using it takes a bit of getting used to sloshing about the arcane byways of the legislative process.

http://thomas.loc.gov

National Autistic Society (NAS)

This is the major autism organization in the United Kingdom. It is the best one-stop site for UK residents. As an American across the pond, I must say I was shocked by the categorical statements and low expectations of several authors of featured articles written for professionals and educators, especially those related to further education. Nevertheless, this site is rich with practical advice, numerous articles, and excellent references to community support services for children and adults.

http://www.oneworld.org/autism_uk/

Autism Society of America (ASA)

This major US autism organization is still recovering from a bad case of organizational blahs. It holds annual conventions but even with a revamping of the national leadership, individuals with AS are still given the organizational stiff shoulder. Many state chapters still don't know what to do with us either. However, the site has some good links, and as a major player on the autism scene in the US, high functioning individuals might want to nip the national organization and its state and local chapters in the heels for recognition.

http://www.autism-society.org/

Asperger web ring home page

Accessing Shelly Cline's website will provide you with the open-sesame to a growing collection of websites authored and maintained by AS individuals. This address provides the surfer with all the information needed to hook into this fascinating collection of sites.

http://aspie.freeservers.com/Asperger.html

Bibliography

Until very recently, materials written about Asperger Syndrome were simply not readable. Even the seminal works of Lorna Wing and Uta Frith were not written for the casual reader. Authors who established their reputations in the field of high functioning autism continue to write professional-level materials that prove a challenge to the lay reader. The majority of these books are written by neurotypical authors. I have chosen most of 'How To' books for their readability and the practicality of their methods. Authors on the autistic spectrum are identified with an asterisk (*).

One book, above all others, must be noted. *Asperger's Syndrome: A Guide for Parents and Professionals* is simply the best book to date on understanding AS. Tony Attwood, an Australian psychologist with over twenty years of experience working with Asperger Syndrome clients – children and adults – presents the clearest, most down-to-earth picture of AS currently on the market. The book is widely available, and among the books listed below, remains a best seller. Simply put, it has become a parents' Bible. Dr Attwood's book should form the underpinnings of a knowledge base by any professional coming in first contact with persons with AS. Dr Attwood is collaborating with Carol Gray ('Social Stories') on a new book – not published as yet – to teach social skills.

Attwood, T. (1997) *Asperger's Syndrome: A Guide for Parents and Professionals.* London: Jessica Kingsley Publishers.

Baron-Cohen, S. (1995) *Mindblindness: An Essay on Autism and Theory of Mind.* Cambridge, MA: MIT Press.

*Choisser, B. (1997) *Face Blind!* An on-line book at *http://www.choisser.com/faceblind/*

Coyne, P., Nyberg, C., Vandenburg, M.L. (1999) *Developing Leisure Time Skills for Persons with Autism: A Practical Approach for Home, School and Community.* Arlington, TX: Future Horizons, Inc.

*Craig, C. G. (1998) *Quality of Life in High Functioning Autistic Adults: Conceptualizing Outcome.* Unpublished PhD dissertation. Los Angeles, CA: Department of Psychology, University of Southern California.

Duke, M.P., Nowicki, S. Jr. and Martin, E.A. (1996) *Teaching Your Child the Language of Social Success.* Atlanta, GA: Peachtree Publishers.

*Durig, A. (1993) *The Microsociology of Autism.* Paper on file with Sociology Department, Indiana University, Bloomington, IN. Also online at ftp://ftp.syr.edu/information/autism/microsocialogy_of_autism.txt

*Durig, A. (1996) *Autism and the Crisis of Meaning.* State University of New York.

Fisher, R., Ury, W. and Patton, B. (eds) (1991) *Getting to YES: Negotiating Agreement Without Giving In*. Second Edition.New York: Penguin Books.

Fouse, B. and Wheeler, M. (1997) *A Treasure Chest of Behavioral Strategies for Individuals with Autism*. Arlington, TX: Future Horizons, Inc.

Green, R.W. (1998) *The Explosive Child: A New Approach for Understanding and Parenting Easily Frustrated, 'Chronically Inflexible' Children*. New York: HarperCollins.

*Holliday Willey, L. (1999) *Pretending to be Normal: Living with Asperger's Syndrome*. London: Jessica Kingsley Publishers.

Klin, A., Volkmar, F. and Sparrow, S. (eds) (2000) *Asperger Syndrome*. New York: The Guilford Press.

Kranowitz, C.S. (1998) *The Out-of-Sync Child: Recognizing and Coping with Sensory Integration Dysfunction*. New York: Berkley Publishing Group.

Lovett, H. (1996) *Learning to Listen: Positive Approaches to People with Difficult Behaviour*. London: Jessica Kingsley Publishers.

Nowicki Jr., S. and Duke, M.P. (1992) *Helping the Child Who Doesn't Fit In*. Atlanta, GA: Peachtree Publishers.

Nadeau, K. G. (1997) *ADD in the Workplace: Choices, Changes and Challenges*. Bristol, PA: Brunner/Mazel, Inc.

O'Brien, J., and Lovett, H. (1992) *Finding a Way Toward Everyday Lives: The Contribution of Person Centered Planning*. Harrisburg, PA: Office of Mental Retardation. *http://soeweb.syr.edu/thechp/everyday.pdf*

*O'Neill, J. L. (1999) *Through the Eyes of Aliens*. London: Jessica Kingsley Publishers.

Pease, A. (1984) *Signals: How to Use Body Language for Power, Success and Love*. New York: Bantam Books.

Pease, A. (1987) *Body Language - How to Read Others' Thoughts by Their Gestures*. Avalon Beach NSW Australia: Camel Publishing Company.

Ratey, J. and Johnson, C. (1997) *Shadow Syndrome*. New York: Pantheon Press.

*Schneider, E. (1999) *Discovering my Autism: Apologia Pro Vita Sua (With Apologies to Cardinal Newman)*. London: Jessica Kingsley Publishers.

Siegel, D.J. (1999) *The Developing Mind: Toward a Neurobiology of Interpersonal Experience*. New York: The Guilford Press.

*Singer, J. (1998) *Odd People In: The Birth of Community Amongst People on the 'Autistic Spectrum'*. Unpublished BA thesis. Sydney, Australia: Faculty of Humanities and Social Science, University of Technology.

Thompson, S. (1997) *The Source for Nonverbal Learning Disorders*. East Moline, IL: Linguisystems, Inc.

Trench, B. M. (1998) *Lifeskills for Vocational Success – A Resource Manual for Trainers in Vocational Rehabilitation Settings*. Birmingham, AL: Workshops, Inc.

Wiles, M.G. (1998) *To What Extent does the Provision of Services Meet the Needs of Autistic People on Leaving School?* Unpublished MSc thesis. Oxford: Department of Applied Social Sciences, University of Oxford.

*Williams, D. (1998) *Autism and Sensing: The Unlost Instinct*. London: Jessica Kingsley Publishers.

Wilmot, W. W., Hocker, J.L. (1998) *Interpersonal Conflict*. Fifth Edition. Boston: McGraw Hill.

Winner, M.G. (2000) *Inside Out: What Makes a Person with Social-Cognitive Deficits Tick? Asperger Syndrome, Non-Verbal Learning Disabilities, High-Functioning Autism, PDD-NOS – The I LAUGH Approach*. Self-Published and available from 4871 Trent Drive, San Jose, CA 95124, (408) 879-0508.

Index